All Write SkillsBook

Workshop Activities, Minilessons, and Daily Sentences

. . . a resource of student workshop activities,
minilessons, and daily sentences to accompany
the *All Write* handbook

WRITE SOURCE®

GREAT SOURCE EDUCATION GROUP
a Houghton Mifflin Company
Wilmington, Massachusetts

A Few Words About the
All Write SkillsBook

Before you begin . . .

The SkillsBook provides you with opportunities to practice the editing and proofreading skills presented in the *All Write* handbook. The handbook contains guidelines, examples, and models to help you complete your work in the SkillsBook. The activities in the SkillsBook are organized into Workshop Activities, Minilessons, and Daily Sentences.

Workshop Activities

The Workshop Activities cover what you need to know to become a better writer and proofreader. In each activity, you will find an introduction to the basic idea and references for the handbook pages you will want to use. Each activity has clear directions and examples. The **Next Step** provides follow-up work.

Minilessons

Each Minilesson covers one idea from the handbook. Most minilessons can be done on your own or with a partner.

Daily Sentences

The Daily Sentences review basic writing skills. Focused Sentences help you concentrate on one editing skill at a time. Proofreading Sentences offer several different sentence problems for you to correct. You may need to cross out a word, insert a punctuation mark, add a capital letter, and so on. Such practice helps you become a more careful writer and a better proofreader.

Authors: Pat Sebranek and Dave Kemper

Trademarks and trade names are shown in this book strictly for illustrative purposes and are the property of their respective owners. The authors' references herein should not be regarded as affecting their validity.

Great Source and **Write Source** are registered trademarks of Houghton Mifflin Company.

Printed in the United States of America

International Standard Book Number: 0-669-49954-4 (student edition)

1 2 3 4 5 6 7 8 9 10 - VHG - 10 09 08 07 06 05 04 03 02

International Standard Book Number: 0-669-49955-2 (teacher edition)

1 2 3 4 5 6 7 8 9 10 - VHG - 10 09 08 07 06 05 04 03 02

Table of Contents

Proofreading Activities

Sentence Activities

Understanding Sentences

Language Activities

The Parts of Speech

Adverbs

Prepositions

Interjections

Conjunctions

Minilessons

Proofreader's Guide Practice

Daily Sentences

Focused Sentences

Proofreading Sentences

Proofreading Activities

Every activity includes a main Practice part, in which you check sentences for punctuation, mechanics, and usage. Some activities also include a Try It Out part, in which you and your classmates can try out a basic proofreading skill or concept *before* you get to the main Practice sentences. In addition, many activities include a Next Step, which gives you follow-up practice with a certain skill.

Using End Punctuation

Periods, question marks, and exclamation points usually signal the end of a sentence. (Refer to "Marking Punctuation" on pages 345-346 in the handbook if you have any questions about using these three punctuation marks.)

[Examples] **Basketball is my favorite sport.**
▲

Samuel, what sport do you like?
▲

"I like all sports!" Samuel shouted.
▲   ▲

Note: In dialogue, you may need to use more than one end mark.

 **Add the correct end punctuation marks in the following sentences. The first sentence has been done for you.**

1. Our coach sent me into the game_·_

2. I was a reserve player on our basketball team___

3. "Why me___" I asked myself___

4. Our coach hollered, "One minute left___"

5. Our team had the ball___

6. Who would get to take the last shot___

7. All of a sudden I felt the ball in my hands___

8. Why did they throw the ball to me___

9. "Shoot the ball___" yelled the crowd___

10. I set up and shot the ball___

11. I heard the buzzer___ I yelled, "No___"

12. The buzzer was my alarm clock___

13. It was all just a dream___

End Punctuation Practice

Periods, question marks, and exclamation points are the three ways to end a sentence. Most of the time, it's easy to know which of these punctuation marks to use. But some sentences are a little harder. (Refer to "Marking Punctuation" on pages 345-346 in the handbook for more information.)

[Examples] **Our class was talking about the Olympics.** ▲

Jerry asked, "Can you imagine being in the Olympics?" ▲

"Awesome!" Carla said. ▲ ▲

 **Add the correct end punctuation marks in the following sentences. The first sentence has been done for you.**

1. Paulo said his cousin was in the Olympics once __·__

2. "Really _____" asked Jerry _____ "What sport did he compete in _____"

3. Paulo said his cousin played football _____

4. "No way _____ That can't be true _____" Jerry said _____

5. Ms. Carrera asked Jerry why it couldn't be true _____

6. Jerry said, "There is no football in the Olympics _____"

7. "There is too _____" Paulo yelled _____

8. Ms. Carrera said, "You're both right _____ Who can explain this mystery _____"

9. Carla said, "The game Americans call soccer is called football in other

    countries _____ Paulo, your cousin played soccer in the Olympics, right _____"

10. "That's right _____ In the Olympics it's called football, but it's the same game

    as soccer _____ "

11. "Why does everything have to be so complicated _____ " Jerry asked _____

Using Commas 1

Commas make writing easier to read by keeping words, numbers, and ideas from running together. (Refer to "Comma" on pages 347-352 in the handbook for more information.)

[Examples] Here are four uses for commas:

- To Keep Numbers Clear
  1,000 soup labels   42,000,000 people

- In Dates and Addresses
  March 1, 2010 (but March 2010)

  My address is 404 State Street, Milwaukee, Wisconsin 50012.

- In Direct Address
  Jakub, please turn in your assignment.

- To Set Off Appositive Phrases
  Mr. Robertson, our band teacher, plays the trumpet.

Try It Out

Add commas as necessary in each of the following sentences.

1. My grandfather's address is 143 Maple Street Greendale OH 42019.

2. I have 1730 cards in my baseball card collection.

3. Julisa you really have a great singing voice.

Write two sentences using commas. In your first sentence, write your address. In your second sentence, use a noun of direct address.

_____

_____

_____

Add commas as needed in the following sentences. (Refer to the four uses of commas explained on the previous page.) The first sentence has been done for you.

1. William H. Seward bought Alaska from Russia in 1867 for $720,000.

2. Alaska the largest state in the United States is more than twice the size of Texas.

3. Juneau Alaska's capital city covers 3108 square miles.

4. Anchorage Alaska's largest city has a population of 260,283.

5. Mohamed did you know that there are more than 20 hours of daylight in an Alaskan summer day?

6. Mount McKinley is the highest peak in Alaska; it rises 20320 feet above sea level.

7. You can learn more about the history of Alaska by writing to the Alaska State Library P.O. Box 110571 Juneau AK 99811-0571.

8. Hawaii the last state to join the United States was admitted into the union on August 21 1959.

9. You may land in Honolulu the largest city in Hawaii if you fly to this state.

10. Visitors receive *leis* special wreaths of flowers when they arrive in Hawaii.

Next Step

Refer to your handbook for the rule on using commas to separate adjectives. Then write an original sentence in which you use a comma (or commas) according to this rule. Share your sentence with a classmate.

Using Commas 2

Commas have many different uses in writing. (Refer to "Comma" on pages 347-350 in the handbook for more information.)

[Examples] Here are four important uses of commas:

- To Separate Introductory Phrases and Clauses
  After running the two-mile race, I needed a drink of water.

- To Separate Items in a Series
  I do the mile run, the high jump, and the long jump.

- To Set Off Interruptions
  However, the mile run is my best event.

- To Separate Independent Clauses in Compound Sentences
  I run every morning, but I never run more than three miles.

Try It Out

Add commas as needed in the following sentences.

1. During my free time I enjoy shopping and going to movies.

2. Kerry and I like to shop together but we don't like the same movies.

3. When I go to a movie I sometimes have to borrow money for my ticket.

4. I usually go to movies with Patrice Marisa or Mansi.

5. In fact Patrice and I went to a movie on Saturday.

6. I had to clean my room wash the dishes and take out the garbage before I could go out.

7. While I enjoy scary movies I like love stories even more.

Carefully read the sentences that follow, and add commas as needed. (Refer to the four uses explained on the previous page. Also refer to page 348 in the handbook for the rule about using commas to set off dialogue.)

1. When I was young I made life difficult for my family.

2. "Lisa has an amazing imagination" said my father.

3. This was true. I could be creative inventive and irritating all at the same time.

4. For instance I always wanted to cook something.

5. After my mother thought about it she decided to let me make something.

6. "You'll be sorry" my dad whispered to her.

7. Yes I hoped to impress them with my first dish—graham-cracker pudding.

8. My brother wouldn't even taste it; he only ate cheeseburgers hot dogs and pizza.

9. As a matter of fact he wouldn't even look at it.

10. Then I said "I've got another idea. Bring me the liverwurst ketchup and mayonnaise."

11. I grabbed all of the new ingredients and everyone else left the kitchen.

12. After I put something together I invited everyone back for a snack.

13. Unfortunately no one wanted to eat my orange-colored liver spread.

14. Before I could serve my father he ran out of the room.

15. My spread was really quite good so I ate most of it myself.

Comma Practice 1

Commas are used to set off an appositive from the rest of the sentence. An appositive is a word or phrase that renames or explains the noun that comes before. (Refer to "Comma" on page 352 in the handbook for examples.)

Use commas to set off the appositives in the sentences below. The first sentence has been done for you.

1. Mr. Smith, our English teacher, directed our class play.

2. Sarah Lane my best friend got the lead in the play.

3. Ms. Evans our art teacher designed the sets.

4. Mr. Hyde the school principal had programs printed.

5. On weekends Mr. Roth the school's custodian helped us build the sets.

6. The *Banner* our school newspaper carried pictures of rehearsals.

7. Mrs. Lane the home economics teacher was in charge of costumes.

8. The members of the cast gave Mr. Smith a gift a beautiful director's chair.

9. Tom our class president presented the chair during the dress rehearsal.

10. The play a romantic comedy was a great success.

Next Step

Write three sentences including appositive phrases. Exchange your sentences with a classmate. Make sure your partner has correctly punctuated his or her appositive phrases.

Comma Practice 2

Use commas between words or phrases in a series and before the connecting word in a compound sentence. See the examples below. (Also refer to "Comma" on pages 347 and 350 in the handbook for explanations and examples of these two uses.)

[**Examples**]   Between Items in a Series

Michelangelo was a sculptor, a painter, and an architect.

In a Compound Sentence

He started with a classical education, and then he became an apprentice to a painter.

 **In the sentences below, add commas between items in a series and between independent clauses. The first sentence has been done for you.**

1. Michelangelo stopped painting, and he began working as a sculptor.

2. Michelangelo's statues are known for their size strength and emotion.

3. The beauty power and grace in his artwork still inspire people.

4. Michelangelo lived in Florence and he met Leonardo da Vinci in that city.

5. He liked to work on large projects but he could not complete them all.

6. Michelangelo started his most famous project, the paintings on the ceiling in the Sistine Chapel, in 1508 and he finished it in 1511.

7. His last paintings were complex in design serious in tone and personal in subject matter.

Next Step

Write a sentence on any subject following the pattern of the last sentence above. Use commas correctly in your sentence.

Comma Practice 3

In the sentences below, add commas to set off longer introductory phrases and clauses and to set off appositive phrases. The first sentence has been done for you.

1. Because of Sweden's large social-security system, Swedes receive free education and free health care.

2. While Sweden covers a large area it is very thinly populated.

3. Stockholm Sweden's capital and largest city is located on the Baltic seacoast.

4. Most Swedes live in Stockholm or in Göteborg and Malmo two other large metropolitan areas in Sweden.

5. In northern Sweden the summer sun shines for 24 hours a day.

6. Sweden a constitutional monarchy has a king as its head of state.

7. Although the king is the head of state the real power in Sweden lies with the parliament and the prime minister.

8. Since the end of World War II Sweden has accepted many immigrants.

9. Sweden is famous for smorgasbord hot and cold foods placed on a table for self-service.

10. Since much of Sweden is covered by forests timber is one of its most valuable resources.

Next Step

Write two sentences about a country of your choice. Follow the pattern in the last two sentences above. Use commas correctly.

Comma Practice 4

Commas are used between independent clauses, between items in a series, and between items in dates and addresses. (Refer to "Comma" on pages 347 and 350 in the handbook for explanations and examples.)

Add commas to the following sentences as needed. The first sentence has been done for you.

1. Benjamin Franklin was born on January 17, 1706, in Boston, Massachusetts.

2. Franklin attended school for only two years yet he gained a great deal of knowledge and wisdom.

3. Mathematics philosophy religion and navigation were some of the subjects he studied on his own.

4. Franklin understood many languages, including French Spanish and German.

5. At age 17, he ran away to Philadelphia Pennsylvania and two years later, he owned his own printing business.

6. He married Deborah Reed on September 1 1730.

7. Many huge fires started in Philadelphia so Franklin helped organize the city's first fire department.

8. Because many streets were unpaved dirty and dark, he started a program to have new paved roads.

9. Franklin helped modernize the postal system and he became deputy postmaster general.

10. The Franklin stove the lightning rod and bifocals were all his inventions.

Using Semicolons and Colons

Periods and commas are used again and again in writing. Other punctuation marks such as the **semicolon (;)** and **colon (:)** are used less often. (Refer to "Semicolon" and "Colon" on pages 353-354 in the handbook for more information.)

[**Examples**]   Here are two uses of semicolons:

● To Join Two Independent Clauses That Are Related
My mom bought a computer; I was excited to use it.
(Each clause can stand alone as a sentence.)

● To Join Two Independent Clauses Connected by a Conjunctive Adverb
Tai wanted to use the computer; however, I got to use it first.
(Words such as *however*, *instead*, and *therefore* are conjunctive adverbs. A comma always follows a conjunctive adverb.)

Here is one use of a colon:

● To Introduce a List
Here are three things you must do to earn an A in reading: read ten books, write two book reports, and give one oral report.

Try It Out

Add a semicolon or colon as needed in each of the following sentences.

1. The following items are needed for a picnic drinks, sandwiches, cups, and plates.

2. Ahmad and Alla are twins however, they don't look alike.

3. Larisa has light, curly hair Marisa has dark, straight hair.

4. The library will be closed this week to check the inventory therefore, no one will be able to check out books.

5. Kerry likes pepperoni pizza Harry will eat only cheese pizza.

Add a colon or semicolon as needed in each of the following sentences. The first sentence has been done for you.

1. This month, the following students have birthdays：David, Midia, and Leo.

2. Midia is having a party however, she is not sure when it will be.

3. Midia is my best friend therefore, I want to buy her a present.

4. We are going to Florida this summer we will be there on my birthday.

5. I want to see three things when we go to Florida the Everglades, Key West, and the Atlantic Ocean beaches.

Write original sentences according to the directions. Share your sentences with your classmates.

Write a sentence in which you use a colon to introduce a list of three or four things.

_____

_____

Write a sentence in which you use a semicolon to join two independent clauses with a conjunctive adverb.

_____

_____

Write a sentence in which you use a semicolon to join two independent clauses without a connecting word.

_____

_____

Semicolons and Colons Practice

To correctly punctuate your writing, you need to know how to use semicolons and colons. (Refer to "Semicolon" and "Colon" on pages 353-354 in the handbook for more information.)

[**Examples**]   Here is another use of semicolons:
● To Separate Groups of Words That Contain Commas
Pilar made necklaces with red, blue, and orange beads; buttons shaped like hearts, stars, and moons; and gold chains.

Try It Out

Add semicolons and colons to the following sentences. If the sentence is correct, write a C on the line. Do not use a colon after a verb or a preposition. Example: Amir speaks English, French, and Farsi.

_____ 1. Rashanda has two flags an American flag and an African flag.

_____ 2. The colors of the African flag are black, green, and red.

_____ 3. Rashanda celebrates three special holidays Harambee, Juneteenth, and Kwanzaa.

_____ 4. She also celebrates the Fourth of July, Thanksgiving, and New Year's Day.

_____ 5. On Harambee people go to dances, art shows, and movies eat black-eyed peas and sweet-potato pie and listen to jazz, blues, and rap music.

_____ 6. On Kwanzaa Rashanda's dad wears a brown, black, and white dashiki an African hat, which is called a kofi and African beads.

Add semicolons and colons as needed in the following sentences. If the sentence is correct as it is written, write a C on the line in front of the sentence.

_____ **1.** English has borrowed words from Spanish, German, Italian, Algonquian, and many other languages.

_____ **2.** The following Spanish words are very similar to English words *el chocolate, la ensalada, el tomate,* and *el vegetal.*

_____ **3.** These American states all have Spanish names Arizona, Colorado, Florida, and Montana.

_____ **4.** English uses the Native American names for opossums, chipmunks, and other animals hickory, pecan, and other trees and kayaks, toboggans, and other things that were first made by Native Americans.

_____ **5.** Here are some English words that come from Asian languages *jungle, pepper, shampoo,* and *tea.*

Write original sentences according to the directions.

1. Write a sentence in which you use a colon to introduce a list of several things.

_____

_____

2. Write a sentence in which you introduce a list of things but do not use a colon.

_____

_____

Punctuating Dialogue

Carrying on a conversation is usually easy. You say something, and then another person says something back. Recording a conversation in writing, however, is not quite as easy. There are specific punctuation rules that must be followed. (Refer to "Quotation Marks" on pages 357-358 in the handbook for more examples.)

[Examples] These sentences show how conversation is punctuated.

"I would like to check out this book," said Carlos.

Enisa asked, "Where do I go to return my book?"

"Ask the librarian," said Ms. Mercado. "She will tell you."

Try It Out

Study each of the following sentences. Then write your own sentences patterned after the samples.

1. "Television has too many commercials," said Dina.

   _____

   _____

2. Fara asked, "Do people actually like all of these commercials?"

   _____

   _____

3. "They're too loud," said Max. "I just push the mute button."

   _____

   _____

Punctuate the following sentences with end marks, commas, and quotation marks. The first sentence has been done for you.

1. "I have a doctor's appointment on Tuesday," said Joan.

2. Maya asked Why do you have to see the doctor

3. I need to get a shot before I go to camp said Joan

4. The camp is my mom's idea Joan added I'm not sure I want to go

5. You'll have fun Maya said There will be all kinds of things to do

6. I hope you're right Joan said

7. Too bad you have to get the shot first Maya said

8. I know what you mean replied Joan I hate getting shots

9. Maya said I bet that once the shot is over, you'll feel better about going to camp

10. Hey Joan exclaimed I hadn't thought of that. You're probably right

11. Do they have horseback riding there Maya asked

12. I don't know. I have to find out more about this camp Joan said

13. Well said Maya excitedly if they have horseback riding, maybe I'll come, too

---

Next Step

Share your work with a classmate. Then write down a conversation between you and a friend, between you and a parent, or between two other people. Make sure to punctuate your sentences correctly.

Dialogue Practice 1

Quotation marks are used to set off the exact words of a speaker from the rest of the sentence. (Refer to "Quotation Marks" on pages 357-358 in the handbook for more information.)

[Examples] In each of these example sentences, the exact words of the speaker are set off by quotation marks.

> **Yoshi asked, "What's for lunch?"**
> **"I hope it's not macaroni and cheese," said Akira. "That stuff is gross."**
> **"Maybe we'll have the salad bar. I like that the best," said Yoshi.**

Add quotation marks in the following sentences. The first sentence has been done for you.

1. Carlos said, "I'm going to the block party. Are you?"

2. Sure, I said. When do you want to go?

3. How about late afternoon? Carlos asked. Can you sleep over at my house?

4. Great idea! I replied. I'll ask my parents if it's okay. Should we ask Joe, too?

5. He won't be able to come, Carlos said.

6. Why not? I asked.

7. He's going to visit his cousin for the weekend, Carlos explained.

8. I said, I hope a good band is playing for the party.

Next Step

Re-create a conversation you and a friend or family member have had about school, sports, books, or movies. Use quotation marks correctly.

Dialogue Practice 2

Quotation marks set off the exact words of a speaker. They also mark the titles of songs, poems, short stories, articles, and other short selections. (Refer to "Quotation Marks" on pages 357-358 in the handbook for more information.)

Add quotation marks as needed in the following sentences. The first sentence has been done for you.

1. Juan asked, "Are you going to the program next week?"

2. Of course, Alberto said. I'm in the program.

3. Wow! Juan responded. I didn't know I was talking to a star.

4. Well, you are, Alberto said. (He was scheduled to dance in a skit and sing White Christmas.)

5. You're not the only star, Juan said. (Juan's band would be playing Silver Bells and Feliz Navidad for the program.)

6. The part I like best is when the whole school sings songs, Alberto said.

7. Yes, that's great, Juan said. After the program a bunch of us are going out to sing carols. Do you want to join us?

8. Sounds like fun, Alberto said. I'll ask my mother if we can all stop at my house after the caroling.

Next Step

Re-create a conversation between yourself and a friend. Make sure to use quotation marks correctly.

Punctuating Titles 1

Use italics (or underlining) for titles of books, plays, magazines, movies, TV programs, record albums, CD's, newspapers, and names of ships and aircraft. Use quotation marks for titles of songs, poems, short stories, chapters, articles, and episodes of TV programs. (Refer to "Quotation Marks" on pages 357-358 and "Italics and Underlining" on page 361 in the handbook for more information.)

[Examples]   **Hatchet by Gary Paulson is my favorite book.**

"The Storm" is a chapter in the book Winter Warning.

 **Punctuate the titles in the following sentences. The first sentence has been done for you.**

1. My brother likes to watch Monday Night Football on television.

2. He also likes to read Sports Illustrated magazine.

3. Last week, we rented the movie Spy Kids.

4. In the book Strange Stories, there is a chapter called Laws and Outlaws.

5. The name of the first American newspaper was Publick Occurences.

6. Daybreak in Alabama is a poem in Selected Poems by Langston Hughes.

7. We sang The Star-Spangled Banner before the basketball game.

8. The song Make New Friends but Keep the Old is one of my favorites.

9. I like to watch Home Improvement on television.

10. We are doing A Christmas Carol for our winter school play.

Punctuating Titles 2

[Examples] I do not like the movie <u>Braveheart</u> because it is violent.

My favorite short story is "To Build a Fire" because it contains a lot of suspense and drama.

 **Practice**

Write a sentence naming your favorite (or least favorite) title for each category listed below. In your sentences, try to explain why you like (or dislike) your selections.

1. (movie)

_____

_____

2. (album or CD)

_____

_____

3. (television show)

_____

_____

4. (book)

_____

_____

5. (song)

_____

_____

Hyphens 1

A hyphen (-) is used to make some compound words and to divide a word at the end of a line. A word may be divided only between syllables. (Refer to "Hyphen" on page 355 in the handbook for an explanation and more examples.)

[Examples] Here are hyphens used in compound words:

nine-year-old car   middle-school classroom   CD-ROM

 **Put hyphens where they are needed in the sentences below. The first one has been done for you.**

1. I have a four‸year‸old sister who likes to play with the dog.

2. Doug ate hard boiled eggs for lunch.

3. Tara put on well worn jeans and a leather jacket.

4. If Marla gets up too early, she is a bad tempered girl.

5. The ill nourished dog looks weak.

[Examples] Here are hyphens used to divide words between syllables:

con-nect   bas-ket-ball
key-board   su-per-mar-ket

Use hyphens to divide the following words into syllables. (Check a dictionary.)

1. window _____   6. computer _____

2. teenager _____   7. calendar _____

3. tearoom _____   8. closet _____

4. hyphen _____   9. plastic _____

5. index _____   10. difficult _____

Hyphens 2

Hyphens are used between the numbers in a fraction that is written as a word. Hyphens are also used with a few prefixes (*all, self, ex, great*) and suffixes (*elect, free*). (Refer to "Hyphen" on pages 355-356 in the handbook for more information.)

[Examples]   **Jeri ate three-fourths of a large pizza!**
She is the all-time champion pizza eater.

   **Put hyphens where they are needed in the sentences below. The first one has been done for you.**

1. One‑fourth of the students in my class are from other countries.

2. Tara gave me one half of her dessert.

3. Our class is doing a unit on self esteem.

4. Each of us will do one third of the project.

5. This school is a smoke free zone.

6. George H. W. Bush and Bill Clinton are ex presidents of the United States.

7. Myra's great grandfather came to our class.

8. Vijay is president elect of the science club.

Next Step

Use hyphens to write sentences according to the directions.

1. Write a sentence using a fraction written as a word.

   _____

2. Write a sentence using a word with the prefix *all, self, ex,* or *great.*

   _____

Apostrophes 1

Apostrophes are used to form contractions and to show ownership or possession. (Refer to "Apostrophe" on pages 359-360 in the handbook for specific explanations and more examples.)

[Examples]   Here are the basic uses of apostrophes:

- To Form Contractions
  don't (do + not)   you're (you + are)

- To Form Singular Possessives
  Petru's jacket   the girl's purse

- To Form Plural Possessives
  the students' lunches   the children's snacks

- To Show Shared Possession
  Christina and Guerdy's play

   **Add apostrophes as needed in the following sentences. Use the examples above as a guide.**

1. David and Jakubs friends love soccer.

2. He doesnt care what the car looks like.

3. Juans hobby is cycling.

4. Hes making his own bicycle.

5. Ismaels car is old and rusty.

6. The two girls best sport is volleyball.

7. Did you see the new jerseys in the mens section of the store?

8. Youll find so many different colors to choose from.

Carefully read the paragraph below. Pay particular attention to the underlined words. Put a line through any of those words that have apostrophe errors. Write the correct word above it. The first underlined word has been checked for you. (Refer to "Apostrophe" on pages 359-360 in the handbook for help.)

Hint: Four additional underlined words contain apostrophe errors.

                  grandmother's
1   My ~~grandmothers'~~ pies made her famous in my town. The towns' local

2   diner that featured her pies was known all over the state of New York. When

3   people ate at the diner, they didn't just order a piece of pie. They ordered a

4   slice of Grandma Gray's home-baked pie. In the summer, I'd walk past the

5   diner window where Grandmas' pies were displayed. Usually there was'nt a

6   single piece of pie left, and that was before the lunch hour had even started.

7   Its lucky I didn't have to count on the diner for some of Grandma's pie. I

8   could just run down the street to my grandparents' house and usually find a

9   freshly baked pie on the kitchen table. I grew up in a pie lover's paradise.

Next Step

Write about your favorite food in three or four sentences that all use apostrophes. Have a classmate check your work.

Apostrophes 2

The possessive of most singular nouns is formed by adding an apostrophe and *s*. (Refer to "Apostrophe" on page 359 in the handbook for more information.)

[**Examples**] **I stepped on my <u>dog's</u> tail.** (The tail belongs to the dog.)

<u>Carmen's</u> story surprised everyone. (The story belongs to Carmen.)

Use the singular possessive form of each of the following words in a sentence. (Use your own paper if you need more room.)

1. pencil

_____

_____

2. coat

_____

_____

3. spider

_____

_____

4. _____ (name of a favorite movie or book character)

_____

5. _____ (name of a favorite singer or actor)

_____

Punctuation Review 1

 **Proofread the sentences below. Add any punctuation that is needed. The first sentence has been done for you.**

1. Baseball player Jackie Robinson, the first African American in major-league baseball, was born in Pasadena, California.

2. He played his first game in the majors on April 15 1947.

3. Robinson was also a great football player he played in college for UCLA.

4. Branch Rickey signed Robinson to his first contract and he was Robinsons great friend for life.

5. Robinson played first base second base third base and the outfield.

6. Of course African Americans were thrilled to have Robinson play.

7. Robinson was known for the following baseball skills baserunning bunting and base stealing.

8. Robinson only played for nine seasons however, he became known as one of the greatest players in the game.

9. Jackie Robinson was elected to the Baseball Hall of Fame in Cooperstown New York.

10. When Robinsons number was retired from baseball he said This is truly one of the greatest moments in my life.

Punctuation Review 2

Proofread the paragraphs below. Draw a line through any mark of punctuation that is used incorrectly; add any needed punctuation. The first sentence has been done for you.

1   I don't really know very much about how computers work, but I

2   recently had some firsthand experience with what happens when they

3   don't work. I was at La Guardia Airport in New York City with my mom

4   and dad. We were standing in line to get tickets for Chicago where we

5   were going to get a connecting flight home to Madison. While we

6   were waiting; I noticed that all the TV monitors announcing arrivals and

7   departures had gone blank.

8   "It's probably just a problem with a computer" said my dad.

9   It turned out to be a pretty big problem because soon an airline

10 official announced that something had damaged a main cable and the

11 airports' entire computer system was down. This meant that all

12 computerized operations were being done manually.

13   The ticket lines, which hadn't been moving very fast anyway, slowed

14 to a crawl. People would move their luggage a few inches set it down

15 and wait!

16   Someone announced that people with immediate flights should move

17 to a special counter to speed their ticketing; but it didn't work. The

18 special line quickly became longer than the other lines.   One flight after

19 another was delayed, half the passengers scheduled for those flights were

20 still waiting in line to get their tickets. The manual ticketing was certainly

21 not a speedy process

22   The airline kept asking people to be patient: but from the comments

23 I heard, most passengers were feeling anything but patient.   My dad

24 however remained his usual calm self.

25   We finally got our tickets and were able to get our flight which had

26 been delayed for two hours.   Although we missed our scheduled

27 connecting flight to Madison; we were lucky enough to get a later flight

28 that night.   So despite computers that didn't compute the trip could

29 have been worse.   We might never have left New York?

Next Step

Write a descriptive paragraph about the computer breakdown from a ticket clerk's point of view. Here's a possible starting point: I was typing away on my computer keyboard when the screen suddenly . . .

Capitalization and Abbreviations

You already know that you must capitalize the first word in a sentence. And you also know about capitalizing the specific names of people and places. But there are additional rules for capitalization that you should know about. (Refer to "Capitalization" on pages 362-366 in the handbook for this information.)

It is also important to know how to use abbreviations, the shortened form of words and phrases. For example, *Dr.* is the abbreviation for *Doctor.* (Refer to "Abbreviations" on pages 369-370 for more information.)

Try It Out

Check each of the following phrases. Correct any errors in capitalization and abbreviation by writing the correct form on the line. If the phrase is correct as stated, leave the line blank. The first one has been done for you.

miss daisy _____Miss Daisy_____   governor Davis _____

cooper school _____   mrs daley _____

italian food _____   President George W. Bush _____

mr Hassan _____   dr. Gomez _____

Revolutionary War _____   on planet earth _____

Mississippi river _____   in September _____

404 Wall street _____   Ms Diaz _____

memorial hall _____   South Africa _____

my Mother _____   Winter season _____

Chicago Bulls _____   levi jeans _____

DISCUSS: Share your work with a classmate. Refer to the handbook if you have any questions about the correctness of any of the examples.

Carefully read each sentence below. Put a line through any letter that is capitalized incorrectly. Check abbreviations for correct punctuation. Make the corrections above each mistake. The first sentence has been done for you. *Hint:* **Go through once and fix everything you are sure about. Then use your handbook to help you make additional corrections.**

     M   G   M

1. m̸s. g̸ordon, our science teacher, is taking us to the Natural History m̸useum in Chicago.

2. The Field Trip was planned for tuesday, but school was closed because of bad weather.

3. Early Wednesday morning, the bus arrived in front of our school, Chute middle school.

4. Dr Mendoza, Ms Nguyen, and my Mother were our chaperones.

5. the bus driver drove South on the Ryan expressway until she got to lake shore drive.

6. Along the way, we saw the Sears tower, soldier field (the name of a stadium), and lake Michigan.

7. When we reached the Museum, the bus driver parked right next to a Blue Van.

8. A Tour Guide named mr. lee showed us the different exhibits; the stone age exhibit was the first one we saw.

9. The exhibits show things from different Continents, including north America, Europe, and Asia.

10. The Natural History museum has tour guides who speak polish, spanish, and french.

Capitalization Practice 1

A proper noun names a specific person, place, thing, or idea. Proper nouns are always capitalized. (Refer to "Capitalization" on page 362 in the handbook for more information.)

 **Change the words that should be capitalized in the sentences below. The first sentence has been done for you.**

1. My cousin ^Wwilliam ^Bbanks had a tryout with the ^Ggreen ^Bbay ^Ppackers.

2. William's dad played with calgary in the canadian football league.

3. Now William's dad is senator banks of texas.

4. William was a star halfback at Mayville high school.

5. He was also a star at one of the state universities in texas.

6. William's team played a game in the alamo dome, a stadium in san antonio.

7. After the season, william won the smith trophy, awarded to the most valuable player on the team.

8. William did not make the team in Green Bay, but he is going to try out for the new york giants next year.

Next Step

Write three sentences that contain at least one or two proper nouns each. *But do not capitalize these nouns.* Exchange your work with a classmate. Add the proper capital letters in each other's sentences.

Capitalization Practice 2

Your handbook lists many different rules for using capital letters. Review these rules before you work on this activity. (Refer to "Capitalization" on pages 362-366 in the handbook.)

The following sentences contain capitalization errors. Some words that *should* be capitalized are not; some words that *should not* be capitalized are. Make the required corrections. The first sentence has been done for you.

1. Wisconsin's nickname is the B̶adger S̶tate, and N̶ew Y̶ork's is the E̶mpire S̶tate.

2. My older brother is taking a course called history 101 in college, and he wrote a paper on abraham lincoln.

3. The new york jets used to play in shea stadium.

4. Danny likes to wear Blue Jeans and Hightop shoes.

5. Sam spent a year in israel studying hebrew.

6. Last summer we visited the southwest and went to a navaho Reservation.

7. In Astronomy class we studied the milky way.

8. During the week, Lake Shore drive is as busy as the Edens expressway.

9. Two of my favorite Historical Periods are the middle ages and the renaissance.

10. William Clinton, the former President, is a member of the democratic party.

Next Step

In the handbook, study the rules for using words like *mother, father, aunt,* and *uncle.* Then write two sentences. In the first sentence, use one of these words as a capitalized name. In the second, use one of the words in a way that does not require a capital letter.

Abbreviation Practice

Abbreviations are shortened forms of words. Look at the examples below. (Also refer to "Abbreviations" on pages 369-370 in the handbook for more explanations and examples.)

[**Examples**] **Mister Brown**   **Doctor Black**   **Main Street**

Mr. Brown   **Dr. Black**   **Main St.**

Match the abbreviation in the first column with the correct word in the second column. The first one has been done for you.

_____d_____ **1.** Rd.   **a.** Drive

_____ **2.** Expy.   **b.** West

_____ **3.** Dr.   **c.** Expressway

_____ **4.** Ct.   **d.** Road

_____ **5.** N.   **e.** North

_____ **6.** W.   **f.** Court

Match the abbreviation in the first column with the correct word or words in the second column.

_____ **7.** etc.   **a.** Doctor of Medicine

_____ **8.** lb   **b.** pound

_____ **9.** M.D.   **c.** page

_____ **10.** oz.   **d.** paid

_____ **11.** pd.   **e.** et cetera (and so forth)

_____ **12.** pg.   **f.** ounce

Plurals 1

To know how to form the plurals of nouns, review the rules in the handbook. (Refer to "Plurals" on pages 367-369 in the handbook for this information.)

Practice   **Write the plural for each of the singular words listed below.**

1. hero _____

2. glove _____

3. trees _____

4. crutch _____

5. deer _____

6. fox _____

7. picture _____

8. dress _____

9. leaf _____

10. rodeo _____

11. city _____

12. bush _____

13. foot _____

14. potato _____

15. sky _____

16. piano _____

17. sheep _____

18. photo _____

19. woman _____

20. cupful _____

21. reef _____

22. story _____

23. toy _____

24. wolf _____

25. turkey _____

26. tooth _____

Next Step

Write five sentences about your favorite holiday or most memorable family gathering. Underline the nouns in your sentences and write S above the singular nouns and write P above the plural nouns. (Make sure that your plurals are formed correctly.)

Plurals 2

In each of the sentences below, fill in the correct plural form for the word in parentheses. The first sentence has been done for you.

1. We could hear the _____echoes_____ across the valley. **(echo)**

2. John starts his new _____ tomorrow. **(class)**

3. We removed hair from the _____ . **(brush)**

4. I sent two _____ this morning. **(fax)**

5. Did the three _____ get printed? **(copy)**

6. The flock of _____ flew past the hunters. **(goose)**

7. The _____ of bread baked a long time. **(loaf)**

8. "Put your _____ on your head!" ordered the police officer. **(hand)**

9. The _____ had long ears. **(donkey)**

10. The _____ in the choir sang off-key. **(alto)**

11. All of my _____ turned out to be correct. **(guess)**

12. Snow covered the _____ . **(roof)**

Next Step

Write sentences using the plural form for each of the following words: *wish, deer, life,* and *library.* Exchange your completed sentences with a classmate. Check the plural forms in each other's sentences.

Plurals 3

Before you work on this activity, review the rules in the handbook for forming plurals. (Refer to "Plurals" on pages 367-369 in the handbook for this information.)

In each of the sentences below, fill in the correct plural form for the words in parentheses. The first sentence has been done for you.

1. Dad put the dirty _____*dishes*_____ in the sink. **(dish)**

2. I like onions and _____ in my salad. **(tomato)**

3. The swarm of large _____ ruined the picnic. **(fly)**

4. People could not talk quietly with so many _____ playing. **(radio)**

5. We had fun watching the _____ at the zoo. **(monkey)**

6. We were amazed at the _____ we saw. **(sight)**

7. I was told to put the _____ by the door. **(box)**

8. They watched the _____ playing. **(child)**

9. The three _____ left at noon. **(wife)**

10. The students didn't clean up their _____ . **(mess)**

11. The battle _____ received a round of applause. **(hero)**

12. I found our _____ in a neighbor's yard. **(puppy)**

Next Step

Write sentences using the plural form for each of the following words: *ray, tooth, secretary,* and *watch.* Exchange your completed sentences with a classmate. Check the plural forms in each other's sentences.

Numbers

This activity gives you practice using numbers in your writing. Some numbers should be written as words—*one, two, three,* etc.—and other numbers should be written as numerals—*10, 15, 75,* etc. (Refer to "Numbers" on page 371 in the handbook for explanations and examples.)

In the sentences below, all of the numbers are written as words. Find all the number words that should be written as numerals and change them. The first sentence has been done for you.

1. Three groups in our class are raising money for our class trip on May ~~nineteenth.~~ 19

2. Our class has twenty two students, but each group has ten members.

3. Eight guests from another class brought the total to thirty students.

4. One group is washing cars for three dollars and fifty cents per car.

5. Another group is selling two hundred jumbo candy bars at two dollars and ten cents each.

6. All the money must be raised by May tenth, two thousand two.

7. The third group is selling magazines at two dollars and fifty cents each.

8. This group will try to sell one hundred magazines by May eleventh.

9. Our advisor said we could call him at five five five-two two one four with questions.

10. The class would like to earn seven hundred and fifty dollars altogether.

Next Step

Write two sentences that use numbers correctly as numerals and two sentences that use numbers correctly as words. Exchange your sentences with a partner. Check the use of numbers in each other's sentences.

Mechanics Review

This activity reviews the rules for using capital letters and numbers and for forming plurals in writing. (Refer to "Editing for Mechanics" on pages 362-371 in the handbook for explanations and examples of these rules.)

Correct the mechanical errors in the following sentences. The errors could be related to capital letters, numbers, or plurals.

1. My grandfather was only eighteen years old when he enlisted to fight in world war II.

2. He fought in the battle of the bulge and was wounded 2 times.

3. He was in berlin and other citys that had been bombed.

4. He saw many heros, on both the American and the german sides.

5. Grandfather said that he dreamed of fresh tomatos all during the War.

6. He still has bad memorys of the war nearly forty years later.

7. My Uncle played football for notre dame university and won several trophys.

8. He gave me a college t-shirt that was about 5 sizes too large.

9. Aunt thelma has two big boxes of photographs about my Uncle's football career.

10. Last week the boy scouts sponsored a basketball game in which all of the players had to ride donkies.

11. One donkey named grumpy threw off his rider about ten times.

12. Mayor adams had bunchs of carrots to feed the animals.

Using the Right Word 1

A challenge for all student writers is using the correct form of words that are commonly confused. For example, the word *your* is often confused with *you're*, and the word *there* is often confused with *their* or *they're*. Whenever you have a question about which word is the *right* one to use, turn to the handbook for help. (Refer to "Commonly Misused Words" on pages 379-394 in the handbook for this information.)

[Example] Here is an example sentence in which *your* is used incorrectly:

Incorrect: **Your not washing the dishes fast enough.**

(*Your* shows possession.)

Correct: **You're not washing the dishes fast enough.**

(*You're* is the contraction for *you are*.)

Try It Out

Read this story as a class. Study each underlined word and decide if it is used correctly. If the word is used incorrectly, cross it out and write the correct word above it.

A few months ago, my aunt <u>red</u> a book called *Diet for a Small Planet.*

The book says it is better to eat <u>fewer</u> meat and more vegetables. Aunt Gina

is <u>all ready</u> a vegetarian (someone who doesn't eat meat), and she wants the

rest of us to choose the same <u>course</u>. Since Aunt Gina does most of the

cooking, we <u>no</u> we have to choose between becoming vegetarian or starving.

<u>Their</u> is really nothing else we can do. Now, when I go <u>too</u> the store, I will

have to <u>buy</u> peanut butter and broccoli instead of hot dogs.

If an underlined word in any of the following sentences is used incorrectly, cross it out and write the correct form of the word above it. If the underlined word is correct, leave it alone. The first sentence has been done for you.

1. teach
   To ~~learn~~ us how to appreciate vegetables, Aunt Gina said we'd plant a window-box garden.

2. We all went to the store to <u>by</u> seeds and small plants.

3. "Let's plant some beans," said Aunt Gina, "because they have <u>a lot</u> of vitamins."

4. Of <u>coarse</u>, beans <u>wood</u> not have been my first choice.

5. I started <u>an</u> tomato plant of my own, <u>too</u>.

6. It was my job <u>too</u> keep the plants watered.

7. I watered the soil until the <u>wholes</u> on the bottom of the window box started to leak.

8. That's how we <u>new</u> the plants had enough water.

9. We set the window box in the kitchen window <u>wear</u> it gets the most sunlight.

10. Then we had to <u>weight</u> for the plants to grow.

11. In less than a <u>weak</u>, we started to <u>sea</u> tiny green shoots.

12. Now my <u>whole</u> family enjoys vegetables.

13. <u>Its</u> great growing <u>hour</u> own food.

Next Step

Use the following pairs of words correctly in sentences: *it's, its; be, bee; fewer, less;* and *bring, take.* Use one pair of words per sentence.

Using the Right Word 2

Your handbook lists many of the words that are commonly misused in writing. (Refer to "Commonly Misused Words" on pages 379-394 in the handbook for this information.)

If an underlined word in any of the following sentences is used incorrectly, cross out the word and write the correct form above it. Do not change a word that is correct. The first sentence has been done for you.

1. A brontosaur was ~~an~~ *a* large plant-eating dinosaur that lived about 150 million years ago.

2. Brontosaurs traveled across <u>planes</u> in <u>herds</u>, living on leaves and grasses.

3. Ginkgo trees were <u>there</u> <u>mane</u> source of food.

4. Brontosaurs were probably <u>vary</u> <u>quiet</u>, like giraffes.

5. A healthy brontosaur's <u>wait</u> was about 30 tons.

6. Although scientists <u>right</u> books about dinosaurs, no <u>won</u> is absolutely sure what dinosaurs were like.

7. Scientists learn about dinosaurs from <u>there</u> remains.

8. <u>One</u> thing they don't <u>know</u> about is the brontosaur's color, although it may have been gray.

9. <u>Its</u> a mystery <u>weather</u> they could run well or just plod along.

10. We'll probably never <u>piece</u> together enough information to answer all of <u>hour</u> questions about brontosaurs <u>ore</u> other dinosaurs.

Using the Right Word 3

Your handbook lists many of the words that are commonly misused in writing. (Refer to "Commonly Misused Words" on pages 379–394 in the handbook for this information.)

If the underlined word in any of the following sentences is used incorrectly, cross out the word and write the correct form above it. Do not change a word if it is correct. The first sentence has been done for you.

1. I was <u>~~vary~~</u> worried about Anna and José both going to Gina's party.
   very

2. I needed <u>too</u> sort out my thoughts, so I wrote a note to Carlos.

3. During the video, in the <u>quite</u> classroom, I <u>past</u> my note to Tom.

4. Tom thought the note was <u>four</u> Carol, and he gave it to her.

5. Carol <u>red</u> it and <u>passed</u> it on to Scott.

6. Scott, <u>who's</u> eyesight was not very good in the dark, gave the note to Mr. Kline.

7. Mr. Kline <u>read</u> it <u>allowed</u>.

8. The note read: "Everybody is thinking <u>sew</u> much about Gina's party. But Anna and José need to get along better. I hope they will have <u>sum</u> peace soon."

9. But here's how Mr. K. <u>red</u> the note: "Today everybody is thinking about Ghana. The animals and people <u>there</u> need help. I hope peace comes soon."

10. I learned that Mr. K. is really nice, because he leaned over and said <u>too</u> me, "<u>You're</u> handwriting is getting better." Then he gave me back my note.

Using the Right Word 4

Your handbook lists many of the words that are commonly misused in writing. (Refer to "Commonly Misused Words" on pages 379-394 in the handbook for this information.)

If the underlined word in any of the following sentences is used incorrectly, cross out the word and write the correct form above it. Do not change a word that is correct.

1. <u>Their</u> is only one class that I do not like in school, and that is gym class.

2. <u>Four</u> the kids who run and jump <u>good</u>, I'm sure <u>its</u> great.

3. But for someone like me, <u>its</u> torture.

4. <u>Beside</u> looking silly in a gym uniform, I'm always picked last when <u>it's</u> time to <u>chose</u> sides.

5. The other kids never <u>leave</u> me have the ball when we play basketball; they say I'm <u>to</u> short to shoot a basket.

6. During softball, I can never hit the ball hard enough to get <u>passed</u> first base.

7. Of <u>coarse</u>, the worst part is trying not <u>too</u> look foolish.

8. I always feel as if I am dragging a <u>led</u> <u>weight</u> around with me during gym class.

9. Whenever I <u>hear</u> the teacher blow that <u>medal</u> whistle, I feel like running away.

10. I would <u>by</u> my way out of this class if the <u>principle</u> would let me.

11. I am looking forward <u>too</u> the end of the school year and <u>know</u> more gym classes.

Using the Right Word Review

Practice

Read the story. If the underlined word is used incorrectly, cross out the word and write the correct form above it. Do not change any word that is correct.

1   When <u>hour</u> neighbor's dog had puppies, I <u>new</u> I'd get to pick <u>won</u> for my

2   own. I looked at all the puppies and decided that the <u>two</u> white pups were

3   the best. I <u>chose</u> the one with the little black paws and freckles. I named him

4   Snooze because <u>their</u> was <u>know</u> other puppy that liked <u>too</u> sleep so much.

5   Snooze was only <u>two</u> <u>weaks</u> old when I picked him out, so I had time to learn

6   about puppies before I brought him home. My dad and I bought some <u>would</u>

7   to build <u>an</u> doghouse. Then my mom said she would <u>learn</u> me how to train

8   my dog to do tricks. We went to the library and got <u>an</u> book about dogs. We

9   <u>red</u> about house-training a dog and about teaching it to sit. Every <u>mourning</u> I

10   would visit Snooze at my neighbor's house. We <u>past</u> the time getting <u>too</u>

11   know each other. <u>By</u> the time Snooze came home, he <u>all ready</u> <u>new</u> how to sit

12   and give me his paw to shake. <u>Accept</u> for all the white hair he leaves on <u>hour</u>

13   beds, Snooze seems to be a great dog.

Next Step

Write a short paragraph about a pet that you have or one that you would like to have. Use the incorrect form for some of the commonly misused words listed in the handbook. Do not underline the words. Exchange your paper with a classmate. Check each other's paper for words that are used incorrectly.

Sentence Activities

Every activity includes a main Practice part, in which you either review, analyze, connect, or combine different sentences. Some activities also include a Try It Out part, in which you and your classmates can try out a basic sentence skill or concept *before* you get to the main Practice section. In addition, many activities include a Next Step, which gives you follow-up practice with a certain skill.

Basic Sentence Patterns 1

Sentences in the English language follow basic patterns. These patterns are listed below in the "Try It Out" activity. (Refer to "Basic Sentence Patterns" on page 67 in the handbook for explanations and examples.)

Try It Out

Write your own sentence for each one of the basic patterns. The first one has been done for you. Share your results with your classmates.

1. Subject + Action Verb

   Johnny runs.

2. Subject + Action Verb + Direct Object

   _____

3. Subject + Action Verb + Indirect Object + Direct Object

   _____

   _____

4. Subject + Action Verb + Direct Object + Object Complement

   _____

   _____

5. Subject + Linking Verb + Predicate Noun

   _____

6. Subject + Linking Verb + Predicate Adjective

   _____

Identify the basic pattern for each of the sentences below.
Use the abbreviated forms of the patterns that follow for
your answers. The first one has been done for you.

S + AV	S + AV + DO + OC
S + AV + DO	S + LV + PN
S + AV + IO + DO	S + LV + PA

1. Office workers use computers. _____S + AV + DO_____

2. Chefs cook. _____

3. Mr. Reynolds is a carpenter. _____

4. Doctors offer patients good advice. _____

5. Some cab drivers are friendly. _____

6. The city gave the company a building permit. _____

7. Ms. Jones called her partner a math genius. _____

8. Firefighters clean their equipment. _____

9. The store owners are brothers. _____

10. The office closed. _____

Next Step

   Write three basic sentences in which the verb comes before the
subject. (Refer to "Basic Sentence Patterns" in your handbook for help.)

1. _____

2. _____

3. _____

Basic Sentence Patterns 2

Sentences in the English language follow basic patterns. Knowing these patterns makes it easier to read and write English correctly. (Refer to "Basic Sentence Patterns" on page 67 in the handbook before you do this activity.)

Identify the basic pattern of each sentence below by labeling the sentence parts. Use the sample sentences on page 67 of the handbook as a guide. The first sentence has been done for you.

     S AV DO
1. I rode my bike.

2. Bianca is our team leader.

3. Mateo hit a home run.

4. Marci was happy.

5. Our teacher gave us a test.

6. Tomas is your brother.

7. Jaime feels sick.

8. We all told jokes.

9. I told Marisa a joke.

10. Jorge's notebook is new.

11. The coach called Zoe an excellent runner.

12. That table is an antique.

13. Shanna looked tired.

14. Luis sent his mother a birthday card.

15. On Wednesdays Hosea plays basketball.

Practice **Write an original sentence for each of the basic patterns.**

1. Subject + Action Verb

_____

_____

2. Subject + Action Verb + Direct Object

_____

_____

3. Subject + Action Verb + Indirect Object + Direct Object

_____

_____

4. Subject + Action Verb + Direct Object + Object Complement

_____

_____

5. Subject + Linking Verb + Predicate Noun

_____

_____

6. Subject + Linking Verb + Predicate Adjective

_____

_____

Simple Subjects and Predicates

All sentences must have a subject and a predicate (verb) to express a complete thought. See the example sentences below. (Also refer to "Basic Parts of a Sentence" on page 66 in the handbook for more information.)

[Examples] In the example sentences, the simple subject is underlined once, and the simple predicate (verb) is underlined twice.

The <u>heart</u> <u>pumps</u> blood to all parts of the body.

Our <u>bodies</u> <u>get</u> oxygen through the blood.

In the following sentences, underline the simple subject with one line and the simple predicate with two lines. The first sentence has been done for you.

1. The <u>heart</u> of an average person <u>is</u> the size of his or her fist.

2. Veins take blood to the heart.

3. Arteries carry blood from the heart.

4. Valves in the heart control the flow of blood.

5. Your heart beats about 70 times a minute.

6. The walls of the heart are a special kind of muscle.

7. A heartbeat is one complete contraction and relaxation of the heart.

8. Heart diseases cause about half the deaths in the United States.

9. The chance of heart disease increases for overweight people.

10. Fatty foods put stress and strain on the heart.

11. A blockage of the coronary artery produces a heart attack.

12. Cardiologists are heart specialists.

Simple Subjects and Predicates Practice

Every sentence has a subject and a predicate. The simple subject is the subject without the words that describe or modify it. The simple predicate is the verb without the words that modify or complete it. (Refer to "Basic Parts of a Sentence" on page 66 in the handbook for more information.)

In each sentence, underline the simple subject with one line and the simple predicate with two lines. The first sentence has been done for you.

1. She aimed at the target.

2. Tom's friend was humorous.

3. So we leaped onto the raft.

4. The new pitcher throws a great fastball.

5. They sat on the bench waiting.

6. Suddenly my father appeared.

7. Bonita hurried through the crowd.

8. A garden separated the two houses.

9. Jolene was the drama award winner because of her hard work and enthusiasm.

10. The young horse, bucking and kicking, galloped into the corral.

11. Mr. Tonn laid his hand on his son's shoulder.

12. Across the horizon, dark clouds began to appear.

13. It made me angry.

14. I closed my eyes.

Compound Subjects and Predicates

A sentence may have a compound subject, a compound predicate (verb), or both. See the examples below. (Also refer to "Compound Subjects and Predicates" on page 66 in the handbook for more examples.)

[Examples] The compound subjects are underlined with one line and the compound predicates (verbs) are underlined with two lines.

Bianca and Elena study together.
(The subject *Bianca* and *Elena* is compound.)

Garon writes stories and illustrates them.
(The verb *writes* and *illustrates* is compound.)

The teachers and students discussed and planned an open house.
(The subject and verb are both compound.)

Underline the simple subject with one line and the simple predicate with two lines. The subject or predicate may or may not be compound. The first sentence has been done for you.

1. Indra and Daru asked their science teacher for extra help.

2. On Saturdays, Toshiro and Akira attend baseball practice.

3. The doctor set the broken bone and placed it in a cast.

4. Our neighborhood store closes at 9 p.m.

5. Jeans and T-shirts look great and feel comfortable.

6. In English class, Yolanda and Paula read out loud.

7. The chef chopped the vegetables and added them to the soup.

8. Most plants need a lot of water and sunlight.

9. A photographer focuses on a subject and then takes a picture.

10. Fruits, grains, and vegetables are part of a healthful diet.

Compound Subjects and Predicates Practice

A sentence may have a compound subject, a compound predicate, or both. (Refer to "Compound Subject" and "Compound Predicate" on page 403 in the handbook for more information.)

All of the following sentences have either a compound subject or a compound predicate. (One sentence has a compound subject and a compound predicate.) Underline each simple subject with one line and each simple predicate with two lines. The first sentence has been done for you.

1. At noon they ate lunch and relaxed before returning to class.

2. Then she opened the magazine and began to read.

3. Grass and weeds grew in the vacant lot.

4. Winter wind and snow had little effect on the mail carrier.

5. Zach and Jake left early and came back late.

6. She jumped up, ran to the phone, and said, "Hello."

7. Tom picked up a baseball and threw it.

8. At half past six last night, Linda and Sue went to the video store.

9. Tom lay awake and waited for the alarm to go off.

10. After the concert, students and their parents headed for the refreshment tables.

11. He reached for a saxophone and began to play a jazz tune.

12. In came all the mud-covered children and tired teachers from recess.

13. He entered the classroom, found his desk, and sat down.

Types of Sentences 1

Read about simple, compound, and complex sentences in the handbook. (Refer to "Types of Sentences" on page 406 and "Combining with Longer Sentences" on page 76 in the handbook.)

Identify the type of each sentence below by writing "simple," "compound," or "complex" on the blank space. The first sentence has been done for you.

1. Jane Addams was a famous American social worker.   *simple*

2. Before she became a social worker, Addams studied medicine in Philadelphia. _____

3. Unfortunately, she had to stop her studying because she had health problems. _____

4. In 1883 and in 1888, Addams visited Europe, and she became interested in caring for the poor. _____

5. On her return, she started the Hull House in Chicago. _____

6. Many people came to the Hull House because they wanted to help the poor. _____

7. Addams became a leader in many reform movements. (*To reform* means "to change or improve.") _____

8. She worked hard for women's rights, and she was an outspoken pacifist. _____

9. A *pacifist* is against the use of war or violence to settle problems. _____

10. Children's rights were also very important to Addams. _____

11. When she was 71, Addams won the Nobel Peace Prize. _____

Types of Sentences 2

 **Practice**

Rewrite each of the following simple sentences. First add an independent clause (another simple sentence) to make a compound sentence. Then add a dependent clause to make a complex sentence. (Refer to "Types of Sentences" on page 406 in the handbook for help.) The first one has been done for you.

1. The baseball team will practice tonight.

    compound: _The baseball team will practice tonight, but four of the_

    players are sick.

    complex: _The baseball team will practice tonight unless more players_

    become sick.

2. Our school has an art show.

    compound: _____

    _____

    complex: _____

    _____

3. My friends and I make our own pizzas.

    compound: _____

    _____

    complex: _____

    _____

Kinds of Sentences 1

There are four kinds of sentences: declarative, interrogative, imperative, and exclamatory. (Refer to "Kinds of Sentences" on page 407 in the handbook for information about these types of sentences.)

[Examples] Declarative
Chavez Ravine is the home of the Los Angeles Dodgers.

Interrogative
How many people does the stadium hold?

Imperative
Take the number 17 bus to the stadium.

Exclamatory
The field looks so green!

Remember a time when you visited an important or exciting place for the first time. You may have visited a baseball stadium, a famous historical building, a spectacular scenic spot, or an exciting theme park. Write one sentence of each kind about your experience.

1. Declarative _____

_____

2. Interrogative _____

_____

3. Imperative _____

_____

4. Exclamatory _____

_____

Kinds of Sentences 2

There are four kinds of sentences: declarative, interrogative, imperative, and exclamatory.   Examples are given below. (Refer to "Kinds of Sentences" on page 407 in the handbook for additional examples.)

[Examples]   Declarative
Challenger and *Voyager* are the names of two space shuttles.

Interrogative
Do you know the names of the astronauts on these flights?

Imperative
Memorize the dates for three other spaceflights.

Exclamatory
Space Control, we have liftoff!

 **Recall your most memorable traveling experience. Write one sentence of each kind about your experience.**

1. Declarative _____

_____

2. Interrogative _____

_____

3. Imperative _____

_____

4. Exclamatory _____

_____

Sentence Fragments 1

A **sentence fragment** is a type of sentence error. A sentence fragment occurs when a group of words is missing either a subject or a verb, or both. (Refer to "Sentence Fragment" on page 68 in the handbook for more information.)

[Examples]

Sentence Fragment: **Left his book at home.**
(The subject is missing.)

Corrected Sentence: **Petru left his book at home.**
(A subject is added.)

Sentence Fragment: **Only a few of my friends.**
(The verb is missing.)

Corrected Sentence: **Only a few of my friends read.**
(A verb is added.)

Sentence Fragment: **Always fun for me.**
(The subject and verb are missing.)

Corrected Sentence: **Reading is always fun for me.**
(A subject and a verb are added.)

Try It Out

If the group of words expresses a complete thought, write S (for sentence) in the blank space. If it does not express a complete thought, write F (for fragment) in the blank space.

_____ **1.** *Escape to Freedom* is an exciting book.

_____ **2.** Another great book.

_____ **3.** Starts in an exciting way.

_____ **4.** To learn about it.

DISCUSS: Think of different ways to correct each sentence fragment. Write down your examples and share them with your classmates.

Write S on the line before each group of words that is a complete sentence. Write F on the line before each group of words that is a sentence fragment. The first one has been done for you.

_____S_____ **1.** Jupiter is the largest planet.

_____ **2.** Is the fifth planet from the sun.

_____ **3.** Jupiter, made of gas and ice, a huge, red ball.

_____ **4.** Jupiter so large that 1,300 Earths could fit inside it.

_____ **5.** Jupiter is a big ball of hot gas like the sun.

_____ **6.** Could have been a star if it had been a little bigger.

_____ **7.** This ball of hot gas, like a huge, raging storm.

_____ **8.** Jupiter has 16 moons.

_____ **9.** Has rings around it like Saturn.

_____ **10.** Jupiter was named after the Roman king of the gods.

Next Step

On your own paper, take each group of words you marked as a fragment and write a complete sentence. Share your work. _Remember:_ Always check your own writing assignments for fragments before you turn them in. You may ask a classmate to check your writing as well.

Sentence Fragments 2

The sentence fragment is a common sentence error. A sentence fragment does not express a complete idea. It is missing a subject, a verb, or both. (Refer to "Sentence Errors" on page 68 in the handbook for examples.)

Each group of words below has a line before it and after it. Write S on the first line if the group of words is a complete sentence, F if it is a fragment. For each fragment, decide what is missing—the subject or the verb—and write that word on the second line. The first one has been done for you.

_____F_____ 1. Ms. Adams with our English class. _____verb_____

_____ 2. Has written several books for young readers. _____

_____ 3. She published her first book in 1980. _____

_____ 4. Called it *Sandy's Secret Day.* _____

_____ 5. Is based on the author's little sister. _____

_____ 6. Her sister is the subject of a book. _____

_____ 7. Next week we will be visited by another writer. _____

_____ 8. Our teacher many writers. _____

_____ 9. My favorite author about true stories. _____

_____ 10. Maybe I a writer someday. _____

Next Step

Rewrite the sentence fragments so that they express complete ideas. Then share your corrected sentences with a classmate.

Sentence Fragments 3

This activity gives you practice correcting sentence fragments. (Refer to "Sentence Errors" on page 68 in the handbook for examples and explanations.)

Each group of words below has a line before it and after it. Write S on the first line if the group of words is a complete sentence or F if it is a fragment. For each fragment, decide what is missing—the subject or the verb—and write that word on the second line. The first one has been done for you.

_____F_____ **1.** Eleanor Roosevelt the wife of President Franklin Roosevelt.

_____*verb*_____

_____ **2.** She became a role model for women. _____

_____ **3.** Made fact-finding trips for her husband. _____

_____ **4.** Mrs. Roosevelt gave many lectures. _____

_____ **5.** For six years, Mrs. Roosevelt a delegate to the United

Nations. _____

_____ **6.** Also fought for equal rights for minorities. _____

_____ **7.** Wrote a newspaper column. _____

_____ **8.** In addition, she several books. _____

Next Step

Rewrite the sentence fragments so that they express complete ideas. Include the necessary capital letters and end punctuation marks. Then share your corrected sentences with a classmate.

Run-On Sentences 1

A **run-on sentence** occurs when two simple sentences are joined without punctuation or without a connecting word such as *and, but, or, so,* or *yet*. (Refer to "Run-on Sentence" on page 68 in your handbook for more information and examples.)

[Example]

Run-On Sentence:
Our solar system contains one star it is called the sun.
(Two sentences are joined without punctuation or a connecting word.)

Corrected Sentences:
Our solar system contains one star. It is called the sun.
(These sentences can be correctly punctuated with a period and a capital letter.)
Our solar system contains one star; it is called the sun.
(Or the sentences can be punctuated with a semicolon.)

Try It Out

**Write RO in the blank space if the group of words is a run-on sentence.
Write S in the blank space if the group of words is a correct sentence.**

_____ **1.** There are nine planets I know about four of them.

_____ **2.** Saturn is the name of one of the planets.

_____ **3.** We studied the planets for a month they are amazing.

_____ **4.** We also studied the moon.

_____ **5.** Earth has only one moon some other planets have

many moons.

DISCUSS: As a class (or in a small group), share your responses to the sentences above. Then discuss ways to correct the run-on sentences. Write the examples on the board so everyone can see them.

Write RO on the line before each run-on sentence. Write S on the line before each correct sentence. Correct each run-on. The first sentence has been done for you.

___RO___ **1.** Mars is the fourth planet from the sun. You can see it

from Earth.

_____ **2.** Mars is only one-seventh the size of Earth.

_____ **3.** Mars glows red and orange it is often called the Red Planet.

_____ **4.** The Romans named Mars after their god of war its red

color reminded them of war.

_____ **5.** Mars has seasons like Earth its days are about 24 hours

long.

_____ **6.** Mars has two moons.

_____ **7.** People used to believe that there were people on Mars

they made up stories about Martians.

_____ **8.** About a hundred years ago, scientists thought they saw

water on Mars.

_____ **9.** In 1964 a spacecraft called _Mariner 4_ went to Mars it took

a lot of pictures.

_____ **10.** Scientists studied the pictures they found no signs of life.

_____ **11.** The pictures did show craters like the ones on our moon.

Run-On Sentences 2

A **run-on sentence** is an error that results when two sentences are joined without punctuation or without a connecting word such as *and, but, or, nor, for, so,* or *yet*. (Refer to "Run-on Sentence" on page 68 in the handbook for another example.)

[**Examples**]   *Run-On Sentence:*
There are many great writers my favorite is Jack London.

Corrected Sentences:
There are many great writers. My favorite is Jack London.
(A period and a capital letter have been added.)

Write RO on the line before each run-on sentence. Then correct the following run-on sentences by dividing them into two sentences. Use correct capitalization and end punctuation in your new sentences. If a sentence is not a run-on, write S on the line before it. The first one has been done for you.

_____RO_____ **1.** Jack London was a very popular writer. He wrote *The Call of the Wild.*

_____ **2.** As a boy, London had to live alone he worked long hours in a factory to support himself.

_____ **3.** As a teenager, London worked on a ship going to Japan.

_____ **4.** London started college he quit to look for gold in Alaska.

_____ **5.** He wrote about survival in the cold of the Yukon London wrote about dogsled teams and wolf packs.

_____ **6.** During his life, he made over a million dollars on his books.

Next Step

Correct the run-on sentences above by using a comma and a connecting word *(and, but, or, so,* or *yet)*. Share your sentences with a classmate.

Comma Splices 1

A **comma splice** is an error that results when two sentences are incorrectly joined with a comma. An end punctuation mark, a semicolon, or a comma *plus* a connecting word should be used between the two sentences. (Refer to "Comma Splice" on page 68 in the handbook for more information.)

[**Examples**] *Comma Splice Sentence:*

I am studying famous poets, I must choose one for a report.

Corrected Sentence:

I am studying famous poets, and I must choose one for a report.
(A comma and the connecting word *and* have been added.)

 **Label the sentences with a comma splice CS. Then correct those sentences by adding a connecting word. If a sentence is correct, write S on the line next to it. The first one has been done for you.**

yet (or) but

_____CS_____ **1.** Emily Dickinson is a famous American poet, ∧only a few of

her poems were published during her lifetime.

_____ **2.** She lived in her parents' home, she wrote her poems there.

_____ **3.** She wrote more than 1,700 poems, she didn't want to

publish them.

_____ **4.** She enjoyed writing about plants and animals, she studied

nature carefully.

_____ **5.** Dickinson saved her poems, they were found after she died.

_____ **6.** Then, the poems were published.

_____ **7.** Emily Dickinson became famous long after her death.

_____ **8.** Her poems might have been lost, that would have been sad.

Comma Splices 2

A **comma splice** occurs when two simple sentences are incorrectly connected with a comma. An end punctuation mark, a semicolon, or a comma *plus* a connecting word should be used between two simple sentences. (Refer to "Comma Splice" on page 68 in the handbook for more information.)

In the groups of words below, write CS in front of each comma splice and put an S in front of each correct sentence. Correct each comma splice with an end punctuation mark. The first two have been done for you.

_____CS_____ **1.** Prometheus was a Greek god. He was said to have created

humans.

_____S_____ **2.** Prometheus had to experiment before he finally made

humans.

_____ **3.** Prometheus was fond of humans, he planned to help them.

_____ **4.** Prometheus helped Zeus defeat Cronus, Zeus then became

king of heaven.

_____ **5.** Prometheus' brother helped him improve the lives of

humans.

_____ **6.** Athene helped Prometheus, she gave him knowledge.

_____ **7.** Prometheus wasn't satisfied with his creation, he wanted to

give humans fire as a present.

_____ **8.** Prometheus made Zeus look silly, Zeus refused to allow

humans to have fire.

_____ **9.** Prometheus planned to disobey Zeus, he was going to give humans fire anyway.

_____ **10.** Prometheus went into the fire chamber, he took some charcoal.

_____ **11.** He took the charcoal to earth and started a big bonfire.

_____ **12.** Humans did not understand fire, Prometheus would have to teach them how to handle the gift.

_____ **13.** Prometheus explained about fire to the humans he showed them how to use water to control fire.

_____ **14.** Prometheus told humans they could cook with fire, he told them they could use fire to keep warm.

_____ **15.** Fire made life better for humans.

_____ **16.** Zeus saw people had terrible new power in their hands, he became very angry.

_____ **17.** He decided to punish Promethus, Zeus used a never-ending torture.

Sentence Errors Review 1

Think about what you have learned. A **sentence fragment** is a group of words that is missing a subject, a verb, or both. A fragment does not express a complete thought. A **run-on sentence** occurs when two simple sentences are joined without punctuation or a connecting word.

Write RO in front of any run-on sentences. Write F in front of any sentence fragments.

_____ **1.** Yesterday, Mark and I hiked into the woods we wanted to have

a picnic lunch.

_____ **2.** Some sandwiches and pop in a school backpack.

_____ **3.** We had to hike two and one-half miles to find a good picnic

spot the main trail in the park is four miles long.

_____ **4.** The trail was hot and dusty we were sweaty, cranky, and thirsty.

_____ **5.** The woods were full of bugs they fell on our hair.

_____ **6.** Totally grossed me out!

_____ **7.** The bugs drove me crazy Mark called me a wimp.

_____ **8.** Picked bugs out of my hair when we rested.

_____ **9.** Certainly not the best place for a picnic lunch.

Next Step

Add your corrections to the above sentences. *Special Challenge:* Imagine it was *you* on the outing with Mark. What else happened? What did you see, hear, and feel? Continue writing about this experience—using complete sentences, of course.

Sentence Errors Review 2

Each of the following examples contains a sentence error. Identify the type of error—F for fragment, RO for run-on, or CS for comma splice—in the blank space. Then correct the error. The first one has been done for you.

_____RO_____ **1.** Walt Whitman wrote a book of poetry called *Leaves of*

                      H

           Grass. he is a famous American poet.

_____ **2.** Seen as the great poet of American democracy.

_____ **3.** Lived in Brooklyn and on Long Island.

_____ **4.** He left school at the age of 11, he worked for a printer.

_____ **5.** Also edited the *Eagle* newspaper.

_____ **6.** The first edition of *Leaves of Grass* came out in 1855,

           Whitman made many changes in later editions of the poems.

_____ **7.** A volunteer nurse during the Civil War.

_____ **8.** Abraham Lincoln's death affected Whitman he wrote a

           poem about the president.

_____ **9.** Whitman traveled a lot, he loved the American landscape.

_____**10.** Walt Whitman died more than 100 years ago he is still

           considered a modern poet.

Next Step

Write an explanation and example for each type of sentence error covered in this activity. Exchange your work with a classmate and check the accuracy of each other's ideas and examples.

Rambling Sentences

If you use too many *and*'s, *but*'s, and *so*'s, your writing may include many **rambling sentences** and be hard to follow. (See "Rambling Sentence" on page 68 in the handbook for more information.)

[Example] *Rambling Sentence:* **I went to the museum last week with my class and we saw the new dinosaur exhibit and it was very exciting but we had to leave before seeing everything.**
(All of the ideas are connected in this rambling sentence.)

Revised Sentences: **I went to the museum last week with my class, and we saw the new dinosaur exhibit. It was very exciting, but we had to leave before seeing everything.**
(The ideas are now expressed in two compound sentences.)

Correct the following rambling sentences by taking out some (but not all) of the *and*'s, *but*'s, and *so*'s. Then fix the capitalization and punctuation as needed.

1. We went up to my grandfather's cabin last weekend and we went fishing on

    Saturday morning and I caught a fish so Dad said he'd cook it for lunch.

2. Then we went swimming in the river and my brother and I took turns

    jumping into the water from a tire swing.

3. My brother would push me hard and I'd jump into the water and then he'd

    yell for me to swim back and push him and we spent all afternoon jumping,

    yelling, and swimming.

4. On Sunday morning, Dad cooked pancakes and thick, crunchy bacon on the

    old wood-burning stove and after we ate we wanted to go swimming again

    but we hiked in the woods instead.

Subject-Verb Agreement 1

To write a sentence correctly, you must make the subject and the verb "agree." This means that if the subject is singular, the verb must be singular. If the subject is plural, the verb must be plural. (Refer to "Sentence Agreement" on pages 69-70 in your handbook for more information. Pay special attention to the section "One Subject.")

 **Practice**

In the following sentences, correct each verb that does not agree with its subject. If the verb agrees with the subject, put a C for correct in front of the sentence. In each sentence, the subject is underlined once, and the verb is underlined twice. The first sentence has been done for you.

_____ 1. Some countries has *have* an official language.

_____ 2. The United States has no official language.

_____ 3. English are the most common language in the United States.

_____ 4. However, many Americans speaks other languages.

_____ 5. Immigrants bring their languages from their home countries.

_____ 6. Spanish are the second most common language.

_____ 7. In our class, some students knows more than one language.

_____ 8. Mohan know English, Hindi, and Marathi.

_____ 9. Marianne uses French at home and English at school.

_____ 10. Her family come from Quebec, Canada.

_____ 11. Canada have two official languages, English and French.

_____ 12. Marianne's grandfather speak only French.

Next Step

Write three or more sentences about people you know and the languages they speak. Make sure your subjects and verbs agree.

Subject-Verb Agreement 2

Making subjects and verbs agree in number can be a challenge when the sentence contains a compound subject. When a compound subject is connected by *and,* use a plural verb. When a compound subject is connected by *or* or *nor,* use either a singular or a plural verb. The verb must agree with the subject closest to the verb. (Refer to "Sentence Agreement" on pages 69-70 in the handbook for more information.)

[Examples] In the example sentences, the subject is underlined once, and the verb is underlined twice.

Felix and Luis attend the same school.

(The plural verb *attend* is correct because the compound subject is connected by *and.*)

Neither Felix nor Luis attends Roosevelt Middle School.

(The singular verb *attends* is correct because the subject closest to the verb is singular.)

Put C in front of the sentences in which the subject and verb agree. Correct the verbs in the sentences in which there is an agreement problem. In each sentence, the subject is underlined once, and the verb is underlined twice. The first sentence has been done for you.

                                              pollute

_____ 1. Cars and factories ~~pollutes~~ the air.

_____ 2. Either buses or subways offers people a cleaner form of

transportation in large cities.

_____ 3. Neither air pollution nor acid rain is easy to control.

_____ 4. Acid rain and smoke harms lakes.

_____ 5. Chemicals and other industrial waste pollutes drinking water.

_____ 6. Business people and homeowners need to protect the

environment.

_____ **7.** Aluminum <u>cans</u> and glass <u>bottles</u> <u>litters</u> our large cities.

_____ **8.** Either <u>cans</u> or <u>bottles</u> <u>is</u> recyclable.

_____ **9.** <u>Newspapers</u> and <u>magazines</u> <u>are</u> recyclable, too.

_____ **10.** Dirty <u>air</u> and littered <u>streets</u> <u>make</u> cities environmentally

unhealthy.

Practice **Use each of the following compound subjects in a sentence. Make sure that the subjects and verbs in your sentences agree.**

1. Parnell and Lamarr

_____

_____

2. Neither science nor math

_____

_____

3. Parks and other public places

_____

_____

4. Either students or teachers

_____

_____

Subject-Verb Agreement 3

When a sentence has a compound subject, it can be a challenge to make the subject and verb agree. A compound subject is made up of two or more simple subjects—Mohammed *and* Ismal. (Refer to "Sentence Agreement" on pages 69-70 in the handbook for more information. Pay special attention to the sections about compound subjects.)

In the following sentences, correct each verb that does not agree with its subject. If the verb agrees with the subject, put a C in front of the sentence. In each sentence the subject is underlined once, and the verb is underlined twice. The first sentence has been done for you.

_____ **1.** My sister and I ~~visits~~ *visit* our cousins every summer.

_____ **2.** Bianca and Benito lives in Mexico.

_____ **3.** Our aunt or her friends take us to different festivals.

_____ **4.** Sometimes my sister or I borrows a dress from Bianca.

_____ **5.** Music and dancing is a big part of the festivals.

_____ **6.** Guitars, trumpets, and maracas are the main instruments.

_____ **7.** *La Raspa* or the *Jarabé* are usually the first dance.

_____ **8.** Either Bianca or Benito is the first one on the dance floor.

_____ **9.** Benito and the other kids dances *La Raspa*.

_____ **10.** Bianca and her boyfriend does the *Jarabé*.

_____ **11.** Bianca or her parents asks the musicians to play a rumba.

Next Step

Think of something that you like to do with your family and friends. Write two sentences about this activity, using compound subjects. Make sure your subjects and verbs agree.

Subject-Verb Agreement 4

In sentences, subjects and verbs must agree in number. That is, a singular verb must be used when the subject in a sentence is singular. A plural verb must be used when the subject in a sentence is plural. (Refer to "Sentence Agreement" on pages 69-70 in the handbook for examples. Pay special attention to the section "Indefinite Pronouns.")

Put a C next to each sentence in which the subject and verb agree. The subjects are underlined with one line, and the verbs are underlined with two. If the subject and verb do not agree, correct the verb. The first two sentences have been done for you.

_____C_____ **1.** My friends meet me every Saturday for a game of softball.

(Both the subject and verb are plural, so they agree.)

                                          ride

_____ **2.** Bill and I always ~~rides~~ our bikes to the field.

(Compound subjects connected by "and" require plural verbs. "Ride" is the plural form of the verb.)

_____ **3.** Everyone wants to be on the winning team.

_____ **4.** Either Sally or Bob like to play in the outfield.

_____ **5.** Sally often bring a large thermos full of cold water.

_____ **6.** Eddie and Nancy usually take the first water break.

_____ **7.** Mindy always wear her lucky sneakers with the red laces.

_____ **8.** Ruth and Mary gets few hits.

_____ **9.** They both swing with their eyes closed.

_____ **10.** Each girl enjoy batting.

_____ **11.** We never keep score during the game.

_____ **12.** Everyone have a good time.

Subject-Verb Agreement 5

The subject and verb in each of your sentences must agree in number. If a subject is singular, the verb must be singular. If a subject is plural, the verb must be plural. (Refer to "Sentence Agreement" on pages 69-70 in the handbook for more information.)

[Examples] In the example sentences, the subject is underlined once, and the verb is underlined twice.

S. E. Hinton is the author of *The Outsiders*.

(The subject and verb agree because they are both singular.)

Two characters are called Ponyboy and Soda Pop.

(The subject and verb agree because they are both plural.)

Check the following sentences for subject-verb agreement. If the subject and verb do not agree, correct the verb. If the subject and verb agree, put a C in front of the sentence.

_____ **1.** *The Outsiders* take place in Tulsa, Oklahoma.

_____ **2.** Ponyboy, Soda Pop, and Darry are brothers in the story.

_____ **3.** Their parents is not alive.

_____ **4.** Ponyboy goes to a local school.

_____ **5.** Johnny and Dally is two of the brothers' friends.

_____ **6.** In part of the story, the boys fight another gang.

_____ **7.** Later, Johnny die in a fire.

_____ **8.** Ponyboy learns from these events.

Next Step

Write five sentences about one of your favorite books or movies. Exchange your work with a classmate. Check each other's sentences for subject-verb agreement.

Other Sentence Problems

Always check for the following four sentence problems: *double subjects, pronoun/antecedent agreement, double negatives,* and *confusing "of" for "have."* (Refer to "Sentence Problems" on pages 71-72 in the handbook for more information.)

[Examples] *Double Subject:* **My two friends they are going to the movie.**
Correct: **My two friends are going to the movie.**

Pronoun/Antecedent Problem:
Lisa and Lauren saw a movie, and she had fun.
Correct: **Lisa and Lauren saw a movie, and they had fun.**

Double Negative: **They didn't have no popcorn.**
Correct: **They didn't have popcorn.**

Confusing "of" for "have": **They should of brought some candy.**
Correct: **They should have brought some candy.**

 **Correct any problems in the following sentences. If the sentence is correct, put a C in front of it. The first sentence has been done for you.**

_____ **1.** Do you know how a bill ~~it~~ becomes a law?

_____ **2.** Representatives in Congress propose laws.

_____ **3.** Sometimes, they don't see no need for a law.

_____ **4.** A bill usually goes through many readings in Congress.

_____ **5.** Congress they must pass the bill by a majority vote.

_____ **6.** If the president he signs the bill, it becomes a law.

_____ **7.** The president and Congress don't always agree on a bill.

_____ **8.** Congress may think that the president should of signed the bill.

_____ **9.** If the president does not sign or veto a bill within 10 days, they

becomes a law.

Other Sentence Problems Practice

When you edit your writing assignments, it's important to check for sentence problems such as *double negatives, double subjects, pronoun / antecedent problems,* and *misplaced modifiers.* (Refer to "Sentence Problems" on pages 71-72 in the handbook for examples and explanations.)

The following sentences contain sentence problems. Correct them by crossing out the word or phrase that is incorrect. You may also need to add a word or phrase to make the sentence correct. The first sentence has been done for you.

I went for a walk with my dog.

1. After doing my math assignment, ~~my dog and I went for a walk~~.

2. Mr. Cutteridge said that if students need help, ~~you~~ should ask for it.

3. Tyson said he did not need no help.

4. Lila she moved here from Trinidad.

5. Each student brought their favorite photograph to class.

6. If Adi had known it was going to snow, he would of dressed warmer.

7. If people get chilled, you are more likely to get sick.

8. The mice squeaked when Akiro brought it more food.

9. Our teacher he speaks English and Spanish.

10. Felix said he never had no pets until he moved to Arizona.

11. Elena could of gone to Venezuela for the summer.

Next Step

Choose a partner. Each of you write two sentences that have sentence problems. Then trade sentences and correct them.

Sentence Combining: Key Words

Combine each of the following sets of sentences using either an adjective or an adverb in your new sentence. The first one has been done for you.

1. Aunt Zoe made liver and onions for dinner. She cooked dinner yesterday. **(adverb)**

   Yesterday, Aunt Zoe made liver and onions for dinner.

2. I like babies. I like them when they are chubby. **(adjective)**

   _____

3. My sister's hair is scary looking. My sister's hair is pink. **(adjective)**

   _____

4. During the emergency, we dialed 911. We dialed quickly. **(adverb)**

   _____

5. My shoes hurt my feet. My shoes are new. **(adjective)**

   _____

6. The fan received the last basketball ticket. The fan was happy. **(adjective)**

   _____

7. Marius ate candy and popcorn. He ate noisily. **(adverb)**

   _____

8. Mr. Wilson walked his dog. Mr. Wilson walked slowly. **(adverb)**

   _____

9. Dimitri's jacket was stolen. His jacket was leather. **(adjective)**

   _____

Sentence Combining: Key Words and Phrases

Ideas from shorter sentences can be combined by using key words and phrases. (Refer to "Combining with Key Words" and "Combining with Phrases" on pages 74-75 in the handbook for examples and explanations.)

Combine the following sets of short sentences. The words in parentheses tell you which method to use. The first one has been done for you.

1. That cookie contains chocolate. That cookie contains walnuts. That cookie contains coconut. **(series of words)**

   That cookie contains chocolate, walnuts, and coconut.

2. John is short. John is funny. John is friendly. **(series of words)**

   _____

3. At basketball practice we try plays. We run on the track. **(compound verb)**

   _____

4. Ms. Pyram visited our school. She's an award-winning journalist. **(appositive phrase)**

   _____

5. Alberto hit a long drive. He hit it to left field. **(prepositional phrase)**

   _____

6. Anne got a new sweater. It's a wool sweater. **(key word)**

   _____

7. Theo helps his father on weekends. Kristo helps his father on weekends, too. **(compound subject)**

   _____

Sentence Combining: Coordinating Conjunctions 1

A simple sentence includes only one independent clause (and states only one complete thought). A compound sentence is made up of two or more simple sentences, usually joined by a comma and a coordinating conjunction—*and, but, or, for, so,* or *yet.* (Refer to "Use Compound Sentences" on page 76 in the handbook for more information.)

Combine the following pairs of sentences into one compound sentence. The first one has been done for you.

1. North America lies above the equator. Australia lies below it.

   North America lies above the equator, and Australia lies below it.

2. Texas covers a lot of territory. Alaska covers even more area.

_____

_____

3. New Guinea is the second-largest island in the world. Few people know this fact.

_____

_____

4. Few people live in Greenland. It is the largest island in the world.

_____

_____

5. Many people live in India. Even more people live in China.

_____

_____

Sentence Combining: Coordinating Conjunctions 2

The conjunctions *and, but, or, nor, for, so,* and *yet* are used to connect words, phrases, and sentences in writing. They help make writing move more smoothly from one idea to the next.

Combine the shorter sentences into one longer sentence. Follow the directions that are given.

1. Earning money is important to Sarah. Playing basketball is important to Sarah. Reading is important to Sarah.

   Use "and" to combine a series of words. _____

   _____

   _____

2. The coaches want to buy new uniforms for the team. They don't have enough money.

   Use "but" to make a compound sentence. _____

   _____

   _____

3. Jesse sells magazines on the weekends. Jesse baby-sits on the weekends.

   Use "or" to create a compound verb. _____

   _____

   _____

4. The workers waited for their trains. The students also waited for their trains.

   Use "and" to create a compound subject. _____

   _____

   _____

Use *and, but, or, nor, for, so,* or *yet* to combine each pair of sentences. More than one conjunction can work in some of these sentences.

1. Kyra makes jewelry. She sells it at the swap meet.

_____

2. Kyra makes earrings out of old beads. Kyra makes earrings out of small stones.

_____

3. Kyra uses a rock tumbler to polish the stones. Her sister Salome uses a rock

tumbler to polish the stones.

_____

_____

4. Kyra would like to make turquoise jewelry. She can't afford to buy turquoise.

_____

_____

5. Kyra will be able to buy some turquoise if she sells all her earrings. She will be

able to buy some turquoise if she gets money for her birthday.

_____

_____

6. Kyra has drawn some designs for turquoise jewelry. She will be ready when she

gets some turquoise!

_____

_____

Sentence Combining: Subordinating Conjunctions 1

You can combine two simple sentences into a complex sentence. A subordinating conjunction is one type of connecting word that is used to create complex sentences. Words such as *after, when, since, because, though,* and *before* are examples of subordinating conjunctions. (Refer to "Subordinating Conjunctions" on page 433 in the handbook for a complete list. See page 76 in the handbook for more about forming a complex sentence.)

Try It Out

Combine the following sets of short sentences into complex sentences. Use the word in parentheses to connect your sentences.

1. Yoshi broke the mile-run record. He trains all of the time. **(because)**

   _____

2. Indra wrote poetry. She had time. **(whenever)**

   _____

3. The rope bridge collapsed. Joe stood and watched. **(as)**

   _____

   _____

4. Mike filled his bike tires with air. He rode to town. **(before)**

   _____

   _____

5. Cyrus ran to the bus stop. He saw how late it was. **(when)**

   _____

   _____

Practice

Combine the two simple sentences into one complex sentence using the conjunction in parentheses. Remember the conjunction can come at the beginning of a complex sentence. (See the information about introductory clauses on page 350 in the handbook.)

1. Atman settled into his favorite fishing spot. The sun came up. **(as)**

   _____

   _____

2. Isabel stopped talking. She heard the teacher coming. **(when)**

   _____

   _____

3. Two feet of snow fell. Cristina made it home anyway. **(although)**

   _____

   _____

4. You're all set for school. You haven't received your schedule. **(unless)**

   _____

   _____

5. Victor checked on the two children. He fell asleep. **(before)**

   _____

   _____

Next Step

Write freely for 5 minutes about what happened yesterday between the time you left school and the time you got home. Then exchange your writing with a classmate. Underline any complex sentences your partner has used.

Sentence Combining: Subordinating Conjunctions 2

One way to combine sentences is to use a subordinating conjunction: *after*, *when*, *since*, *because*, *before*, etc. The new combined sentence is called a complex sentence. (Refer to "Combining with Longer Sentences" on page 76 in the handbook for examples.)

Combine each pair of sentences to make a complex sentence. Use the subordinating conjunction that is in parentheses after each pair. The first one has been done for you.

Note: Often the subordinating conjunction will be placed between the two sentences; sometimes it will be placed at the beginning of the new sentence.

1. Scientists study mummies. Mummies provide information about ancient people. **(because)**

   Scientists study mummies because mummies provide information

   about ancient people.

2. Mummies have been found all over the world. Egypt is the country best known for them. **(while)**

   _____

   _____

3. Mummies were buried with food, tools, and games. People thought these things would be needed in the next world. **(because)**

   _____

   _____

4. China's first emperor died in 210 B.C.E. Nearly 8,000 clay soldiers and horses were buried with him. **(after)**

   _____

   _____

Combine the following pairs of sentences to make complex sentences. Use a subordinating conjunction to make each new sentence. (For a list of subordinating conjunctions, refer to "Common Conjunctions" on page 433 in the handbook.) The first one has been done for you. (Answers will vary.)

1. Lord Carnarvon and Howard Carter discovered King Tut's tomb. They had searched for it for two years.

   Lord Carnarvon and Howard Carter discovered King Tut's tomb after

   they had searched for it for two years.

2. They had almost given up. Then one of the men found a door to the tomb.

   _____

   _____

3. They found gold, jewels, and other treasures. They found the mummy of King Tut.

   _____

   _____

4. They had found the treasure. They thought it was theirs.

   _____

   _____

5. But Lord Carnarvon never got any treasure. He died mysteriously the next day.

   _____

   _____

6. Some said the tomb was cursed. People who dug it up often died within one year.

   _____

   _____

Sentence Combining: Relative Pronouns 1

You can combine two simple sentences into a complex sentence using relative pronouns—words such as *who, which,* or *that.* Using these words will help you cut down on repeating words or phrases in your writing. (Refer to "Combining with Longer Sentences" on page 76 in your handbook for more information.)

[Example]

The radio station played unfamiliar songs.

The radio station was geared for an older audience.
(Two simple sentences)

Use the word *which* to combine the sentences.

The radio station, which was geared for an older audience, played unfamiliar songs.
(By combining the two sentences with the word *which,* you avoid repeating *radio station* and create a smooth-reading, longer sentence.)

Try It Out

Combine the following pairs of simple sentences into one complex sentence. In each pair, a relative pronoun, other key words, and punctuation marks have been put into place. The first one has been done for you.

1. The bald-headed mail carrier delivers on Mondays.
   The bald-headed mail carrier is my uncle.

   The bald-headed mail carrier who <u>delivers mail on Mondays</u>

   is <u>my uncle</u> .

2. The cook looks sad and weary.
   He works at the corner coffee shop.

   The cook who _____

   looks _____ .

Combine the simple sentences into one complex sentence. A relative pronoun, other key words, and punctuation marks have been put into place.

1. The black convertible was dented by hail.
   The black convertible parked in the driveway.

   The black convertible, which _____ ,

   was dented _____ .

2. The painting was stolen.
   It was on exhibit in the museum.

   The painting that _____

   was _____ .

3. Pluto is the most distant planet in our solar system.
   It takes 248 years to orbit the sun.

   Pluto, which _____ ,

   is _____ .

4. The extreme heat affected the runners.
   The runners were participating in the relays.

   The extreme heat _____

   who were _____ .

Next Step

Look in the handbook index under "Who/which/that" to find out when to use each of these words. Discuss the examples above with a classmate.

Sentence Combining: Relative Pronouns 2

You can combine two simple sentences into a complex sentence using relative pronouns—*who, whose, which,* and *that.* (Refer to "Combining with Longer Sentences" on page 76 in the handbook for examples.)

Combine the following pairs of sentences to make complex sentences. Use a relative pronoun to connect the sentences. (Refer to the bottom of handbook page 352 for help with punctuation.) The first one has been done for you.

1. Korean immigrants often open produce stands in America. They had been farmers in Korea.

   Korean immigrants who had been farmers in Korea often open

   produce stands in America.

2. Immigrant students work hard in school. They value education.

   _____

   _____

3. The Castro Revolution caused a wave of Cuban immigration to America. The Castro Revolution took over the Cuban government in 1959.

   _____

   _____

4. Irish Americans are found throughout the United States. Their ancestors came here for economic reasons.

   _____

   _____

Next Step

Write two complex sentences of your own using relative pronouns. Share your sentences with a classmate.

Sentence Combining: Review

Now that you've practiced combining sentences, you know that combining can make your writing smoother and more interesting. Review pages 73-76 in your handbook and get ready to put your practice to work.

Rewrite the following paragraphs on the lines below. Combine short, choppy sentences into longer, smoother ones, using the different methods you have already learned about. (Use your own paper if you need more room.)

There was a house. It looked ancient. It was painted white. The paint was faded. The paint was peeling. The roof had holes. Water leaked through the holes. The house had a front porch. The porch was collapsing. The floorboards were rotten. The house and porch looked as though they were suffering from some terrible disease.

Just then an old man appeared. He appeared on the porch. He looked very frail. He looked sick. His hair was faded. His hair looked like the paint on the house. He was sad looking. He belonged in this house.

_____

_____

_____

_____

_____

_____

_____

_____

Changing Sentence Beginnings

If too many of your sentences start with the same word or words, your writing may sound dull. You can correct this problem by changing some of your sentence beginnings. (Refer to "Editing for Sentence Style" on page 63 in the handbook for more information.)

In the following paragraph, all the sentences start in the same way. On the lines below, rewrite the paragraph so at least two or three sentences have different beginnings. (Use your own paper if you need more room.)

Mr. Korcinski came to the United States from Poland. Mr. Korcinski arrived in this country in 1914 when he was only 14 years old. Mr. Korcinski enlisted in the army during World War I. Mr. Korcinski also enlisted in the merchant marines during World War II. Mr. Korcinski sent medicine to his family in Poland while both wars were fought. Mr. Korcinski sold hot dogs at the beach before he opened a popular steak house.

_____

_____

_____

_____

_____

_____

_____

_____

_____

_____

Using Powerful Words

Specific nouns and verbs and strong modifiers help make your writing come alive. They give your writing style. (Refer to "Using Strong, Colorful Words" on page 110 in the handbook for more information.)

Rewrite the following sentences, replacing the underlined words with more specific words or phrases. The first sentence has been done for you.

1. My little brother <u>ran</u> in and out of the <u>room</u>.

   My little brother **darted** in and out of the **kitchen**.

2. The book had a <u>neat</u> ending.

   _____

3. The <u>boy</u> <u>ate</u> his lunch in two minutes.

   _____

4. The <u>basketball player</u> <u>jumped</u> toward the basket.

   _____

5. The <u>dessert</u> tastes <u>good</u>.

   _____

6. We sent my grandmother a <u>nice</u> <u>plant</u>.

   _____

7. The <u>car</u> began making a <u>noise</u>.

   _____

8. The <u>room</u> is a <u>mess</u>.

   _____

Editing for Smoothness and Clarity

Transitions such as *finally, however,* and *also* help tie ideas together. These linking words will make your writing smoother and clearer. Transitions can be used to . . .

- show location,
- indicate time,
- compare two things,
- set off differences,
- emphasize a point,
- summarize ideas, and
- add information.

(Refer to page 88 in the handbook for a list of transitions.)

[**Example**] Read this sentence:

My sister and I argue all the time.

In your writing, you might want to give an example or add more information:

We argue about whose turn it is to do the dishes.

The transition *for example* smoothly links these two thoughts:

My sister and I argue all the time. For example, we argue about whose turn it is to do the dishes.

Try It Out

Use the following linking words to fill in the blanks below.

before   **as soon as**   **finally**

My sister tried to go ice-skating yesterday. _____ she got to the

rink, she tried the main door, but it was locked. She checked another door

_____ she decided to leave. _____ , she called to

get a ride home.

Use the following transitions or linking words to fill in the blanks below. The first one has been done for you.

as soon as   finally   before

moreover   for instance   in fact

although

1   My parents and I get along pretty well, _____ although _____

2   there are some things we disagree about. _____ ,

3   I think my curfew is too early (7 p.m.), but my parents won't change it. One

4   day I explained to them why I should be able to stay out later: "My best friend

5   can stay out till 8 p.m. _____ , everyone I know can

6   stay out later than I can. _____ , I am very

7   responsible and would not get into trouble if I did stay out later.

8   _____ , being able to stay out later would make me

9   more mature. And that is something you are always telling me I should be."

10   _____ I finished my explanation, my father said

11   he'd make my curfew 5:30 p.m. if I didn't stop bugging him about it.

12   _____ , I talked about my curfew all the time—but not

13   any more. After all, 7 p.m. is a whole lot better than 5:30!

Next Step

     Write a short paragraph about someone you know or have read about.
Use at least two or three linking words in your paragraph.

Language Activities

Every activity includes a main Practice part, in which you learn about the different parts of speech. Some activities also include a Try It Out part, in which you and your classmates can try out a basic language skill or concept *before* you get to the main Practice section. In addition, many activities include a Next Step, which gives you follow-up practice with a certain skill or concept.

Using Nouns

Nouns name people, places, things, or ideas. Notice the underlined nouns in the sentence that follows:

Bob throws a **football** with great **accuracy**.

The noun "Bob" names a person, "football" names a thing, and "accuracy" names an idea. (Refer to "Nouns" on page 409 in the handbook for more information.)

Note: The noun "Bob" is also the subject of the sample sentence. The subject usually tells you who or what is doing the action in the sentence.

Try It Out

Underline the nouns used as simple subjects in the sentences that follow. Tell whether each subject (noun) is a person, a place, a thing, or an idea in the space provided. The first sentence has been done for you.

_____idea_____   **1.** The <u>thought</u> of playing football made Bob nervous.

_____   **2.** His teammates studied their nervous quarterback.

_____   **3.** His feelings were perfectly clear to the team.

_____   **4.** A referee blew the whistle for the first down.

_____   **5.** The ball was placed on the 30-yard line.

_____   **6.** Bob ran onto the field with his team.

_____   **7.** The sidelines were filled with cheering fans.

_____   **8.** An opposing player tackled Bob on the first play.

_____   **9.** The hard tackle ended his nervousness.

_____   **10.** Bob leaped to his feet and grinned at the tackler.

Look at the list of words. They are all nouns. Write them under the correct category heading. Three of the nouns have been listed for you.

girls	school	Paul	books	sadness
thought	backpacks	downtown	farm	teachers
first floor	principal	laugh	Carol	glasses
museum	dinosaurs	hugeness	tickets	friendliness

People	Places	Things	Ideas
girls		books	sadness

Next Step

Look around the classroom. Write three nouns that name people, three that name places, three that name things, and three that name ideas. Share your words with a classmate.

Singular and Plural Nouns

A singular noun names one person, place, thing, or idea. A plural noun names more than one person, place, thing, or idea.

Underline all the nouns in the sentences that follow. Write S above each singular noun and P above each plural noun. The number of nouns in each sentence is listed in parentheses. The first sentence has been done for you.

1. The County Fair held every August is the biggest event of the year. (4)

2. The fair is always held in Gouverneur, a small town in New York. (4)

3. People from the town set up the fair and serve the food. (4)

4. In just one day, the parking lots next to the high school are turned into a glittering playground. (4)

5. The fair is jammed with games and exhibits. (3)

6. It's a good idea to ride the Tilt-A-Whirl or the Octopus before eating. (3)

7. There are many different races and games in the afternoon. (3)

8. At night, professional singers and musicians give concerts. (4)

9. Farmers compete for prizes and ribbons with their animals and vegetables. (5)

10. Litter and happy memories remain when the fair is over. (3)

11. The whole town helps clean the parking lots after the fair. (3)

12. After a few weeks, people begin planning the next fair. (3)

Next Step

Write a short paragraph about a festival, fair, circus, or carnival you have attended. Underline the nouns in your writing.

Common and Proper Nouns

A **common noun** is any noun that does not name a specific person, place, thing, or idea. A **proper noun** does name a specific person, place, thing, or idea. Proper nouns are capitalized. Common nouns are not capitalized.

Underline each noun in the sentences below. The number of nouns in each sentence is in parentheses. Write C above each common noun, and put P above each proper noun. (Refer to "Nouns" on page 409 in the handbook for an explanation.) The first sentence has been done for you.

     P   C   P   C

1. <u>Bob</u> buys most of his <u>comics</u> from <u>Komix Variety Store</u> near his <u>house</u>. (4)

2. To protect his collection, Bob places each comic book in a plastic bag. (4)

3. Bob collects comic books for fun. (3)

4. When Bob's dad was a boy, he also collected comics. (3)

5. Bob's dad gave him a selection of comics published during World War II. (4)

6. Aquaman, Sub-Mariner, and G.I. Joe are Bob's favorite superheroes. (4)

7. The best comics have exciting stories and good illustrations. (3)

Next Step

Apply your knowledge of common and proper nouns in two acrostic poems. The subject for one poem should be a common noun, and the subject for the second should be a proper noun. (Refer to "Acrostic Poetry" on page 177 in your handbook for a model.)

Share your poems with a classmate. Discuss which parts you like in each other's poems. Also discuss any questions you have. (You may want to make some changes in your work after this discussion.)

General and Specific Nouns

Good writers know the value of using specific nouns to create effective word pictures for readers. Read the two columns of nouns that follow:

General	Specific
instrument	microscope
dog	poodle
game	volleyball
pitch	fastball
fiction	novel

The specific nouns are much clearer and more interesting than the general nouns.

Practice **Write down four general nouns. Use each word as the heading for a separate list. Then see how many examples of specific nouns you can list under each heading.**

_____ _____ _____ _____

_____ _____ _____ _____

_____ _____ _____ _____

_____ _____ _____ _____

_____ _____ _____ _____

_____ _____ _____ _____

Next Step

After sharing lists, choose one noun you find interesting. Use that noun as the start of a clustering exercise. (Refer to "Clustering" in the handbook index for guidelines and a model.)

Count and Noncount Nouns 1

Count nouns can have *a, an,* or *one* in front of them. They have a plural form. Noncount nouns cannot have *a, an,* or *one* in front of them. They do not have a special plural form. (Refer to "Count and Noncount Nouns" on page 411 in your handbook for examples.)

Try It Out

Underline the noncount nouns in the following sentences.

1. The <u>snow</u> sparkles like <u>sugar</u>.

2. Mohan had fun at the party.

3. We heard thunder.

4. The sleet turns into ice on the roads.

5. I got money to buy milk.

6. Raoul's family got new furniture.

One noun is underlined in each of the following sentences. If the noun is used as a count noun, write a C in the blank. If the noun is used as a noncount noun, write an N in the blank. The first two sentences have been done for you.

    N   **1.** Luis bleached his <u>hair</u> blond.

    C   **2.** Dad made a face when he found a cat <u>hair</u> in his coffee.

_____ **3.** Dad brought home fried <u>chicken</u> for dinner.

_____ **4.** Liza asked if she could borrow some <u>paper</u>.

_____ **5.** My Aunt Dolores has a pet <u>chicken</u>.

_____ **6.** The morning <u>light</u> wakes me at about 6:30.

_____ **7.** Theo told me to turn on a <u>light</u>.

_____ **8.** Every December we put <u>lights</u> on our trees.

Count and Noncount Nouns 2

This activity gives you more practice identifying count and noncount nouns. (Refer to "Count and Noncount Nouns" on page 411 in the handbook for examples.)

 **Each sentence below contains one count noun and one noncount noun. Underline each count noun, and circle each noncount noun. The first sentence has been done for you.**

1. We bought (flour) for the cookies.

2. I got sand in my shoes.

3. My clothes are in the dryer.

4. There is dirt on the floor.

5. Our parents bought us some clothes.

6. I have money, but only a few dollars.

7. We need new furniture, especially chairs.

8. That family has good luck.

9. My homework is two reading assignments.

10. We used snow to build a fort.

Next Step

Use each of the following noncount nouns correctly in a sentence.

clothes _____

_____

sand _____

_____

Count and Noncount Nouns 3

This activity gives you more practice identifying count and noncount nouns. (Refer to "Count and Noncount Nouns" on page 411 in the handbook for examples.)

In the sentences below, underline the count nouns, and circle the noncount nouns. The first sentence has been done for you.

1. The ⟨drizzle⟩ made the ⟨air⟩ feel even colder.

2. The puppies are playing in the mud.

3. My parents check my homework.

4. Your assignment is on your desk.

5. I hear laughter coming from the boys' room.

6. They are watching television.

7. They have a television in their room.

8. Thunder and lightning continued until daylight.

9. How much money did you spend to have your hair cut?

10. Who got mud on the rug?

Next Step

Think of a noun that can be used as a count noun or as a noncount noun. Write two sentences, one using the noun as a count noun, the other using it as a noncount noun.

_____

_____

_____

Uses of Nouns 1

Nouns can be used in different ways in sentences. Three uses are given below. (Refer to "Uses of Nouns" on page 412 in the handbook for more information.)

[Examples] *Subject Noun:* **Students enter the cafeteria.**

(A subject noun is the part of the sentence that does something or is being talked about.)

Predicate Noun: **Math is my favorite class.**

(A predicate noun follows a linking verb—*is, are, was, were,* etc.— and renames the subject.)

Possessive Noun: **Petru's locker won't open.**

(A possessive noun shows ownership.)

Try It Out

Label the underlined nouns in the following sentences on the blanks provided. Write SN for subject noun, PN for predicate noun, and POS for possessive noun. The first sentence has been done for you.

_____PN_____ **1.** She is a computer <u>expert</u>.

_____ **2.** <u>Dea</u> memorized the names of the 50 states.

_____ **3.** He left his book on <u>Mr. Tran's</u> desk.

_____ **4.** Hannah was an <u>alto</u> in the choir.

_____ **5.** Some <u>cars</u> run on solar energy.

_____ **6.** Juan followed his <u>teacher's</u> advice.

_____ **7.** Gina will be the first <u>runner</u> in the relay.

_____ **8.** The <u>racers</u> warmed up before the meet.

In the following sentences, label the underlined nouns. Write SN above the noun if it is a subject noun, PN if it is a predicate noun, and POS if it is a possessive noun. The first sentence has been done for you.

    SN   PN

1. Marisa was the next speaker.

2. The boys' coach looked surprised.

3. Monday is the worst day of the week.

4. Hopeton's dogs barked loudly.

5. The teacher read Larisa's poem out loud.

6. Guerdy and Kerry are loyal friends.

7. Yesterday, Eduardo met Danny's father.

8. My grandparents are great singers.

9. The last report was, by far, our hardest assignment.

10. Ms. Vega's car is a red convertible.

Next Step

    Write three sentences about your lunchtime in school. Besides subject nouns, include at least one possessive noun and one predicate noun in your writing. Label each noun (subject noun, possessive noun, predicate noun) just as you did in the practice activity above. After you have completed your sentences, have a partner check your labels.

Uses of Nouns 2

In certain cases, nouns are used as objects. Three types of object nouns are given below. (Refer to object nouns on page 412, direct objects and indirect objects on page 424, and prepositional phrases on page 432 in the handbook for more information.)

[**Examples**] *Direct Object:* **Richard sent a funny letter.**

(A direct object answers the question *what?* or *whom?* after an action verb.)

Indirect Object: **Richard sent Danny a funny letter.**

(An indirect object names the person *to whom* or *for whom* something is done. It comes after the action verb but before the direct object.)

Object of Preposition: **Richard sent a funny letter in the mail.**

(An object of the preposition is the noun or pronoun at the end of a prepositional phrase. *In the mail* is a prepositional phrase.)

Try It Out

Label the underlined nouns in the following sentences on the blanks provided. Write DO for direct object, IO for indirect object, and OP for object of the preposition. The first sentence has been done for you.

_____IO_____ **1.** Danny showed his <u>sister</u> the letter.

_____ **2.** She ripped open the <u>envelope</u>.

_____ **3.** The funny story in the <u>letter</u> made them laugh.

_____ **4.** Then Danny wrote <u>Richard</u> a letter.

_____ **5.** He put it in a mailbox near his <u>house</u>.

_____ **6.** Richard received the <u>letter</u> two days later.

In the following sentences, label the underlined nouns. Write DO above the noun if it is a direct object, IO if it is an indirect object, and OP if it is an object of the preposition. The first sentence has been done for you.

1. The group of <u>students</u> entered the singing <u>contest</u>.
   (OP above students, DO above contest)

2. Christina gave each <u>friend</u> a warm <u>hug</u>.

3. The man slipped the <u>wallet</u> into his back <u>pocket</u>.

4. Officer Lee offered the young <u>man</u> a second <u>chance</u>.

5. You hear many strange <u>noises</u> at <u>night</u>.

6. Our librarian sent <u>Adnan</u> a <u>note</u> about an overdue <u>book</u>.

7. Ms. Daley put the <u>papers</u> in her <u>briefcase</u>.

8. Commuters on the <u>subway</u> read <u>newspapers</u>.

9. The mechanic showed my <u>dad</u> the broken <u>hose</u>.

10. David threw the <u>football</u> to <u>Harris</u>.

11. After <u>school</u> Von ran on the <u>treadmill</u>.

12. Natasha gave her <u>friend</u> a <u>ring</u> for her <u>birthday</u>.

13. Stay at the <u>gym</u> until <u>noon</u>.

14. Show <u>Sheila</u> the <u>directions</u> to the <u>theater</u>.

Next Step

Write three sentences about one of your best or one of your worst days. Each sentence should contain a noun used as a different kind of object. (Your sentences may contain more than one kind of object.) Label the objects, just as you did in the activity above. After you complete your sentences, have a partner check your labels.

Using Pronouns 1

Pronouns take the place of or substitute for nouns. The example below shows how very important pronouns can be.

[Example]

Without Pronouns:
Larisa decided Larisa would study Larisa's math book.
(The sentence sounds clumsy.)

With Pronouns:
Larisa decided she would study her math book.
(The pronouns "she" and "her" make the sentence easier to read.)

Note: Personal pronouns are the most common type of pronouns. They include words like *I, we, he, her, they, you,* etc. (Refer to "Pronouns" on page 414 in the handbook for a complete list.)

Try It Out

Substitute a pronoun for each underlined noun.

Sasha wanted to give <u>Sasha's</u> bike to <u>Sasha's</u> friend.

_____

Grandmother told Rick that <u>Rick</u> must do <u>Rick's</u> own homework.

_____

Did you replace the underlined "Sasha's" with the pronoun "her"?

Sasha wanted to give <u>her</u> bike to <u>her</u> friend.

Did you replace the underlined "Rick" with the pronoun "he" and "Rick's" with the pronoun "his"?

Grandmother told Rick that <u>he</u> must do <u>his</u> own homework.

Underline the personal pronouns in the following sentences. The number of personal pronouns in each sentence is given in parentheses. The first sentence has been done for you.

1. <u>My</u> friend and <u>I</u> asked Mr. Simon if <u>we</u> could borrow <u>his</u> boat. (4)

2. We asked Mr. Simon if he wanted to go fishing with us. (3)

3. Mr. Simon told us that he was busy, but he would let us use his boat. (5)

4. My friend got into the boat first. (1)

5. I followed her into it. (3)

6. We rowed the boat out into the water where we could fish. (2)

7. I grabbed the hook, but it got stuck in my finger. (3)

8. My friend helped me get the hook out of my finger. (3)

9. We baited our hooks and started to fish. (2)

10. After about 15 minutes, I finally caught my first fish. (2)

Write three more sentences telling about the adventures in the boat. Be sure to use pronouns.

1. _____

   _____

2. _____

   _____

3. _____

   _____

Using Pronouns 2

Pronouns are words that are used in place of nouns. By correctly using pronouns, you can avoid unnecessary repetition and write smoother, more interesting sentences.

Examples   *A sentence without pronouns:*

The coach thought the coach should diagram the coach's new play on the board.

(Repeating the noun "coach" creates an awkward sentence.)

The same sentence with pronouns:

The coach thought <u>he</u> should diagram <u>his</u> new play on the board.

(Substituting the pronouns "he" and "his" for "coach" and "coach's" creates a smooth-reading sentence.)

Most of the pronouns you use are *personal pronouns* (*I, we, they, he, her,* etc.), but there are other types of pronouns as well. (Refer to "Pronouns" on page 413 in the handbook for additional explanations and examples.)

Underline the personal pronouns in the following sentences. (The number of personal pronouns in each sentence is given in parentheses.) The first sentence has been done for you.

1. John decided to write a book about <u>his</u> family members. (1)

2. They were eager to see how he would describe them. (3)

3. John finished the first two chapters; he showed them to his family. (3)

4. His relatives were angry with him. (2)

5. His aunt said he made her sound like a mean person. (3)

6. John's mother said she was mad at him. (2)

7. John's sister said he should forget about writing his book. (2)

Pronouns and Antecedents

The word the pronoun replaces is called the **antecedent.** If the antecedent is singular, the pronoun must be singular. If the antecedent is plural, the pronoun must be plural. (Refer to "Antecedents" on page 413 in the handbook for more information.)

Underline the correct pronoun or pronouns in parentheses. Then draw an arrow to the pronoun's antecedent. The first sentence has been done for you.

1. Everyone should try to improve (his or her/their) grades.

2. The soldiers were awarded (his/their) medals.

3. If a player works hard, (he or she/they) may be chosen captain.

4. Each store offered (its/their) employees a discount.

5. Both schools offered (its/their) students a good education.

6. The student worked to increase (his or her/their) reading comprehension.

7. Bill and John displayed (his/their) winning science project.

8. Either Claudia or Larisa entered (her/their) writing in the contest.

9. Sefton gave Ms. Jones the assignment before (she/they) expected it.

10. All of the players hope that the new coach will help (him or her/them) improve.

Next Step

Write at least five sentences about a fun time you had with family or friends. Before you share your writing, check your sentences for pronoun-antecedent agreement errors.

Person of a Pronoun 1

Personal pronouns are either first person, second person, or third person. (Refer to "Person of Pronouns" on page 414 in the handbook for more information. Pay special attention to the chart of personal pronouns.)

[Examples]   *First Person:* **I like jokes.** (The pronoun *I* is speaking.)

Second Person: **You like stories.** (The pronoun *you* is spoken to.)

Third Person: **They like comics.** (The pronoun *they* is spoken about.)

Underline the personal pronouns in the following sentences. Then write a 1, 2, or 3 above each pronoun to show whether it is a first-person pronoun, a second-person pronoun, or a third-person pronoun. The first sentence has been done for you.

1. Julisa lives next door to me, and I like her.
       (1)   (1)   (3)

2. Do you want to come with us to Fara's house?

3. I will call my parents, and they will pick us up.

4. Tell the neighbors that their cat is in our yard.

5. Are you sure that cat is theirs?

6. Yes, I watch Henry for my neighbors.

7. Are those books yours or hers?

8. The books are hers, but the video is mine.

9. We found Indra's gloves under your coat.

10. Tell Gerrod to get his book and take it home.

11. He thinks he lost it.

12. I called you, but your mom said you were asleep.

Person of a Pronoun 2

Point of view refers to the position or angle from which a story is told. The person of a pronoun shows the point of view in a story. A story can be told from the **first-person** point of view, the **second-person** point of view, or the **third-person** point of view. (Refer to "Person of Pronouns" on page 414 in the handbook for more information.)

Read the first paragraph of "Unwanted Solo" on page 130 in the handbook. Katie Broitman, writing about herself, used the first-person pronouns "I" and "my." The paragraph is written in the first-person point of view.

Rewrite the paragraph using second-person pronouns *(you, your)* **instead of first-person pronouns. Imagine that you are writing to Katie to remind her about her "unwanted solo." Your paragraph will be written in the second-person point of view.**

_____

_____

_____

_____

Rewrite the paragraph using third-person pronouns *(she, her)*. **Now you are telling a classmate about Katie's "unwanted solo." This paragraph will be written in the third-person point of view. (Hint: The first helping verb must also change.)**

_____

_____

_____

_____

Next Step

Rewrite a paragraph in one of your own narratives or stories, changing the point of view from first person to third person.

Using Verbs

Swing, shimmy, and *shuffle* are strong **action verbs.** Words such as these can make your writing more effective. For example, a form of the verb "swing" creates a clear picture in the following sentence:

[Example] **Bob *swung* Amy off her feet during the first dance.**

("Swung" is an action verb.)

Not all verbs express action. Words like *is, are, was,* and *were* are called **linking verbs** because they "link" subjects to nouns or adjectives.

[Example] **Amy and Bob *are* perfect dance partners.**

("Are" is a linking verb, connecting the compound subject "Amy and Bob" with the noun "partners.")

Try It Out

Underline the verbs in the following sentences with two lines. Label each action verb A and each linking verb L. (Refer to "Linking Verbs" on page 417 in the handbook for a list of these verbs.) The first sentence has been done for you.

1. The janitor <u>opened</u> the gym door for the dance.
                A

2. The dance was the first one of the school year.

3. The dance started slowly.

4. Mrs. Jones, our gym teacher, dragged Eduardo out onto the floor.

5. Then other students joined them.

6. Christine and David were the best dancers.

7. Adnan danced a waltz with Mrs. Taylor, our principal.

8. She is a very good dancer.

9. The dance ended at 8:00 p.m.

Auxiliary or helping verbs come before main verbs. Forms of *be, has,* and *do* are commonly used as auxiliary verbs. (Refer to "Helping Verbs" on page 417 in the handbook.) In each of the following sentences, underline the helping verbs and main verbs with two lines. All but two of the sentences contain auxiliary or helping verbs. The first sentence has been done for you.

1. The dance <u>was promoted</u> very effectively.

2. The first dance of the year was considered an important event by students.

3. Mrs. Taylor and Mrs. Jones had supervised many dances in the past.

4. They have enjoyed dances for a long time.

5. Only a few students knew the latest dance steps.

6. Few of the students had danced before.

7. Mrs. Taylor showed everyone an easy way to "slow dance."

8. She has helped many students in the past.

9. The disc jockey did play a variety of music.

10. By the end of the night, almost all of the students had danced at least once.

Next Step

Write three sentences about a subject of your choice. Use a form of the auxiliary verb "be" in one of your sentences, a form of the auxiliary verb "has" in another sentence, and a form of the auxiliary verb "do" in your final sentence.

Types of Verbs

A verb shows action or links the subject to another word in the sentence. Action verbs tell what the subject is doing. Linking verbs link a subject to a noun or an adjective. Helping verbs help the main verb.

Read the following sentences and note the underlined verbs. Decide whether the verbs are action verbs (A), linking verbs (L), or helping verbs (H). Write the correct letter above each verb. (Refer to "Types of Verbs" on page 417 in the handbook for examples.) The first sentence has been done for you.

1. Our cat Soot <u>was</u> [L] a skinny, homeless stray until he <u>adopted</u> [A] us.

2. One morning I <u>opened</u> the back door, and Soot <u>strolled</u> into the kitchen.

3. The kitchen quickly <u>became</u> his favorite room.

4. Soot <u>leaves</u> the kitchen only for emergencies.

5. He even <u>sleeps</u> in the kitchen, curled up next to his food.

6. I <u>have</u> seen him on the kitchen counter.

7. Soot <u>has</u> grown much heavier.

8. Soot <u>eats</u> too much.

9. Soot <u>should</u> go on a diet.

10. It <u>will</u> be hard for Soot to diet.

Next Step

Write three sentences about an animal that is not usually a pet. Use an action verb in one of your sentences, a linking verb in another sentence, and a helping verb in the other sentence.

Modal Verbs 1

Modal verbs help the main verb express meaning. Words such as *can, could,* and *might* are modals. (Refer to "Types of Verbs" on page 417 in the handbook for more information.)

In the sentences below, circle the modal verbs and underline the main verbs with two lines. (They are not always next to each other!) The first sentence has been done for you.

1. We (have to) leave early tomorrow, so we (can) finish our project.

2. Maybe we ought to ask Dad to drive us.

3. Okay, I will ask him tonight.

4. Dad, would you drive Dimitri and me to school tomorrow?

5. I would do it, but then I might be late for work.

6. Well, we have got to leave early anyway.

7. Can you be ready at 7:00?

8. Yes, we could set an alarm, but we may sleep through it!

9. Will you knock on our door at 6:30, just in case?

10. Okay, but you must be ready on time.

11. We will be ready, because we have to complete our project.

Next Step

Review the meanings and sample sentences for the modal *may* on page 418 in the handbook. Then close your book and write two sentences. In your first sentence, use *may* to express a possibility. In your second sentence, use *may* to express a request. Exchange your work with a partner and discuss each other's sentences.

Modal Verbs 2

In this activity you will practice working with modal verbs. (Study the table of "Common Modal Verbs" on page 418 in your handbook.)

Practice

Below is a list of modal verbs. Match each modal verb to its meaning. Write the letter of the correct meaning next to each verb. Some letters will be used more than once.

1. ought to _____
2. might _____
3. have got to _____
4. can _____
5. must _____
6. will _____
7. may _____
8. have to _____
9. would _____

a. expresses a strong need
b. expresses a possibility
c. expresses an ability
d. expresses an intent
e. expresses a feeling of duty
f. expresses a desire

Write three sentences; in each one, use a different modal from the list above.

_____

_____

_____

_____

_____

Next Step

Review the meanings and sample sentences for the modal *could* on page 418. Then write two sentences. In your first sentence, use *could* to express an ability. In your second sentence, use *could* to express a possibility. Exchange your work with a partner and discuss each other's sentences.

Helping Verbs 1

A **helping verb** "helps" the main verb express time, action, meaning, etc. The helping verb comes before the main verb. See the examples below. (Also refer to "Types of Verbs" on page 417 in the handbook for more information.)

[Examples]   In these sentences, the helping verbs are circled, and the main verbs are underlined.

Lee ⟨is⟩ looking for his guinea pig.

Patches ⟨has⟩ escaped before, and Lee ⟨has⟩ always found him.

Here are some verbs that often act as helping verbs:

am, are, is, was, were, do, does, did, have, has, had

Each of the following sentences has one helping verb and one main verb. (They are not always next to each other!) Circle each helping verb and underline each main verb with two lines.

1. I ⟨am⟩ attending a Juneteenth celebration next month.

2. Juneteenth is celebrated on June 19.

3. In Galveston, Texas, slavery was abolished on that day in 1865.

4. All the slaves in that area were freed.

5. I did not know about this holiday before.

6. Here in Washington, a celebration is held at the Smithsonian Institution.

7. Lamarr and his family are taking me to the parade and the play.

8. Before last year, Lamarr had never seen the play about Harriet Tubman.

Next Step

Write three sentences about holidays or celebrations. Use helping verbs in your sentences.

Helping Verbs 2

Helping verbs include *has, had* and *have; do* and *did;* and forms of the verb "be" (*is, am, was, were,* etc.). **Helping verbs** add information about the action or the time of the main verb. (Refer to "Types of Verbs" on page 417 in the handbook for more information.)

Note: Verbs that act as helping verbs can also stand alone as main verbs.

[Examples] Zoe (**was**) talking.

"Was" is the helping verb; "talking" is the main verb.

Zoe (**was**) happy.

"Was" is the main verb; "happy" is an adjective, not a verb.

Open your handbook to "America's Civil War" on page 272. On the lines below, write the helping verbs that are used in the selection. Next to each helping verb, write the main verb that goes with it. The first one has been done for you.

	Helping Verb	Main Verb		Helping Verb	Main Verb
1.	was	elected	3.		
2.			4.		

Remember: Verbs that are helping verbs can also be main verbs. In four sentences, the verbs *was* and *were* are used as main verbs. Copy those sentences on the lines below. Circle the main verb. The first one has been done for you.

1. Because Lincoln (was) against the spread of slavery, . . .

2. _____

_____

3. _____

_____

_____

4. _____

Two-Word Verbs

This activity gives you practice identifying two-word verbs. (Refer to "Common Two-Word Verbs" on page 426 in the handbook for examples.)

Fill in the blank in each sentence below with a form of one of the following two-word verbs. The first sentence has been done for you.

write down	**leave out**	**break down**
clear out	**pick out**	**call off**
fill out	**call up**	**put on**

1. My mom _____ called off _____ my dentist's appointment.

2. Chefs never _____ the key ingredients in their cooking.

3. Everyone _____ of the building when the alarm sounded.

4. Lamarr's mother _____ the freshest vegetables for her soups.

5. After Athena's father gets in his car, he _____ his seat belt.

6. Yolanda _____ the application for the job at the day-care center.

7. Grant wanted to _____ his friend before the game started.

8. Everyone _____ the due date for the essay assignment.

Next Step

Write sentences using the following two-word verbs. Check in your handbook if you're not sure of the meaning of any of the verbs.

1. hang up _____

_____

2. mix up _____

_____

Simple Verb Tenses

The **present tense** of a verb states an action that is happening now or that happens regularly. The **past tense** of a verb states an action that happened at a specific time in the past. The **future tense** of a verb states an action that will take place in the future. (Refer to "Tenses of Verbs" on page 419 in the handbook for more information.)

[Examples]   *Present Tense:* **Yolanda lives in El Paso.**

Past Tense: **When she was little, she lived in Juarez.**

Future Tense: **Someday she will live in Los Angeles.**

Write three sentences about your life. First, write a sentence about your life now, using a present-tense verb. Next, write a sentence about your life in the past, using a past-tense verb. Finally, write a sentence about your life in the future, using a future-tense verb.

Your life now (present-tense verb):

_____

_____

Your life in the past (past-tense verb):

_____

_____

Your life in the future (future-tense verb):

_____

_____

Underline the verb or verbs in each sentence with two lines. Then, on the line after the sentence, write *present*, *past*, or *future*. The first sentence has been done for you.

1. Each and every one of us has many personal values. __present__

2. The workers used 40 railcars full of supplies. _____

3. As usual, I want to get A's in all of my classes. _____

4. Bobcat jumped down the rocks. _____

5. My family and I will begin planning my Quinceanera. _____

6. He still plays with his 28 grandchildren and 20 great-grandchildren. _____

7. Wilma Mankiller was the first woman chief of the Cherokee nation. _____

8. The choir toured the United States for a year. _____

9. I will always value education, my culture, and the power of love. _____

10. I will start by telling about my mother. _____

11. I felt like melting into the stage. _____

Next Step

Go back to the sentence that you wrote about your life now. Rewrite this sentence putting the verb in the past tense. Then rewrite your sentence about your life in the past putting the verb in the present tense.

Simple and Perfect Tenses

Verb tenses indicate time. The *simple tenses* show whether an event takes place in the present, past, or future.

The *perfect tenses* show special relationships between events and time.

- The *present perfect tense* expresses an action that began in the past but continues in the present.
- The *past perfect tense* expresses an action that began and was completed in the past.
- And the *future perfect tense* states an action that will begin and end at a specific time in the future.

(Refer to "Tenses of Verbs" on page 419 in your handbook for more information.)

For each of the verbs that follow, write sentences using the tenses asked for. The first one has been done for you.

do

I *do* crossword puzzles.

(present)

I *did* two crossword puzzles.

(past)

By Friday, I will have *done* six crossword puzzles.

(future perfect)

eat

(future)

(present perfect)

(present)

wear

_____

(present)

_____

(past)

_____

(future perfect)

grow

_____

(future)

_____

(present perfect)

_____

(present)

_____

(your choice)

_____

(future)

_____

(past perfect)

_____

(present)

Next Step

As a class, take turns writing some of your sentences on the board. Identify the verb in each sentence and decide if its tense is correct.

Irregular Verbs 1

Some verbs in the English language are irregular. Most **irregular verbs** do not end in *ed* when used in the past tense or when used with *has, have,* or *had*. Instead of adding *ed*, the word usually changes. (Refer to "Common Irregular Verbs" on pages 422-423 in the handbook for a list of these verbs.)

[Examples] Study these irregular verbs. Read and repeat the principal parts of these verbs to yourself several times.

Present Tense	Past Tense	Past Participle
blow	blew	blown
drink	drank	drunk
draw	drew	drawn
give	gave	given
hide	hid	hidden
weave	wove	woven
tear	tore	torn
shake	shook	shaken
ride	rode	ridden

Try It Out

Carefully study the irregular verbs on this page. Then cover them with a sheet of paper, and write the principal parts for the verbs below. Check your work by uncovering the words above.

Present Tense	Past Tense	Past Participle
drink		
draw		
give		
hide		
shake		
ride		

Carefully study the chart of irregular verbs in your hand-book; then fill in the blank spaces below. Have your handbook closed as you do the work. Refer to it only after you have finished. Share your results with a classmate.

	Present Tense	Past Tense	Past Participle
1.	run	ran	
2.	lay		
3.		flew	
4.	throw		
5.			worn
6.		came	come
7.	spring		
8.	freeze	froze	
9.			sung
10.	ring		
11.		shrank	
12.		rose	
13.	shine	shone	
14.	grow		

Next Step

Write five sentences in which you misuse some of the irregular verbs used in this exercise. Exchange your paper with a classmate. Correct the misused verbs in each other's sentences. (Refer to the handbook to check for accuracy.)

Irregular Verbs 2

The spelling of some irregular verbs doesn't change when you state a past action or use *has, have,* or *had* with the verb. A list of some of these irregular verbs follows. (See "Common Irregular Verbs" on pages 422-423 in the handbook for a more complete list of irregular verbs.)

[Examples]

Present Tense	Past Tense	Past Participle
set	set	set
burst	burst	burst
cost	cost	cost
cut	cut	cut
hit	hit	hit
hurt	hurt	hurt
let	let	let
put	put	put
spread	spread	spread

Remember: When one of these verbs is used with a third-person singular noun in the present tense, you must add an *s* to the verb:

[Examples]

I can't buy that denim jacket. It costs too much money.

("Costs" is a third-person singular verb in the present tense.)

Fill in the missing sentence for each irregular verb listed. Your sentences must use the verb according to the principal part stated in the parentheses. The first one has been done for you.

1. burst

(present tense) _The water pipe often bursts in cold weather._

(past tense) _The water pipe burst in cold weather._

(past participle) _The water pipe has burst in cold weather._

2. cut

(present tense) Gerald never cuts any classes.

(past tense) _____

(past participle) Gerald has never cut any classes.

3. set

(present tense) _____

(past tense) Yoshi set the table for dinner.

(past participle) Yoshi had set the table for dinner.

4. let

(present tense) Some teachers let us talk during our writing time.

(past tense) _____

(past participle) Some teachers have let us talk during our writing time.

5. spread

(present tense) The cooks spread butter on all of the rolls.

(past tense) The cooks spread butter on all of the rolls.

(past participle) _____

Next Step

There is one irregular verb—*read*—that is spelled the same in all of its principal parts, but it is pronounced differently in the present tense than it is in the other parts. (In the present, the vowel sound is long—*rēd*. In the past and past participle, the vowel sound is short—*rĕd*.) Write three sentences using this verb in its three principal parts. Then read your sentences aloud.

Irregular Verbs 3

To make the past tense and the past participle of regular verbs, you add *ed* to the verb (*walk–walked–had walked*). But irregular verbs are different. They don't use the regular *ed* ending to make those two forms. That's why they're called irregular. Review the irregular verbs listed in the handbook. (Refer to "Common Irregular Verbs" on pages 422-423 in the handbook for this list.)

In each sentence below, underline the irregular verb. Then, on the lines, write the past tense and the past participle of the verb. (Remember that the past participle is used with the helping verbs *has, have,* or *had.*) The first one has been done for you. Close your handbook for this activity.

	Past Tense	Past Participle (with *has, have,* or *had*)
1. We begin at noon.	began	begun
2. I bring cookies.		
3. My friends buy sandwiches.		
4. She catches the softball.		
5. He draws pictures.		
6. They eat lunch.		
7. She knows the answers.		
8. I run around the track.		
9. We swim in the pool.		
10. We wake up early.		

Next Step

Check your work using the handbook. Then write sentences using the past tense and past participle of the verbs in sentences 3 and 5 above.

Irregular Verb Review

This review gives you more practice using the different forms of irregular verbs. (Refer to "Common Irregular Verbs" on pages 422-423 in the handbook for a listing of irregular verbs.)

Each sentence below has at least one underlined verb that is stated incorrectly. Cross out each of these underlined verbs and write the correct form above it. The first sentence has been done for you. (*Note:* Keep your handbook closed for this review.)

1. When we got to the softball field, we ~~choosed~~ *chose* teams.

2. While we were choosing sides, I <u>seen</u> someone I knew from school.

3. Jacquetta was already on third base when Hector <u>getted</u> a hit.

4. On the next pitch, Hector <u>stealed</u> second base.

5. Hiro <u>hitted</u> the ball, but the right fielder <u>catched</u> it.

6. After the catch, Jacquetta <u>run</u> to home plate, and Hector <u>run</u> toward third.

7. Before we <u>knowed</u> what had happened, Hector was on the ground.

8. A bee had <u>flew</u> around his head while he was running.

9. He limped over to the bleachers and <u>sit</u> down.

10. Hector asked me if he had <u>breaked</u> his leg, but I didn't think so.

11. I <u>taked</u> him some water, and he <u>drunk</u> it.

12. Then Hector's sister <u>telled</u> their mom about the bee.

Next Step

Now check your work using the list of irregular verbs in your handbook. Correct your mistakes.

Using Adjectives

Adjectives modify nouns and pronouns in sentences. Adjectives usually answer questions like *how many?* (*six* cookies), *what kind?* (*oatmeal* cookies), *which one?* (*that* cookie), and so on. (Refer to "Adjectives" on page 427 in your handbook for more information.)

Underline the adjectives in the following sentences. (The number of adjectives in each sentence is indicated in parentheses.) *Note:* **Do not underline the articles *a, an,* and *the* in this exercise. The first sentence has been done for you.**

1. John liked to escape the <u>polluted</u> city for the <u>clean</u> air of the wilderness. (2)

2. Convincing Charlie to explore nature was not an easy job. (1)

3. A determined John finally persuaded Charlie to try a camping trip. (2)

4. Charlie was not sure exchanging a large apartment for a tiny tent was a great idea. (3)

5. Charlie wanted to pack a portable stove, a folding chair, and a hammock. (2)

6. John told Charlie not to bring the three items. (1)

7. The two friends drove to the hiking trail that led to the campground. (2)

8. On the trail they met a fat porcupine. (1)

9. They also saw a delicate fawn drinking from a clear stream. (2)

10. Charlie commented on the scenic view of a distant valley. (2)

11. That night they sat around a flickering fire and told funny stories. (3)

12. In the morning they took a brisk swim in the frigid lake. (2)

13. They spotted a sleek otter in the lake. (1)

14. Charlie thanked John for a great time as they headed back to the city. (1)

A Closer Look at Adjectives

The adjectives you use should be colorful, but they should also help express the right feeling, or *connotation,* in your writing. (Refer to "connotation" on the top of page 111 in the handbook for more information.)

Fill in each of the blanks below with one of the two words listed after the paragraph. Choose the word that best expresses the right meaning and feeling. (The two italicized words in the first sentence set the tone for the rest of the paragraph.)

My room at home is a *peaceful* and *secure* place.   It is my own special

space of (**1**) _____ harmony, especially in contrast to the chaos that

exists outside my door. I view my room as a (**2**) _____ spot where I

can rest after a rough day at school. Everything in the room has a calming

effect on me, including my books, my music, and the (**3**) _____ pastel

colors. Everyone needs a (**4**) _____ retreat, a place to think and

regroup before facing the (**5**) _____ routine of life. My room is that

place of (**6**) _____ for me.

1. **sleepy, tranquil**	4. **private, lonely**
2. **mild, soothing**	5. **habitual, everyday**
3. **gentle, bland**	6. **ease, comfort**

Next Step

Write three or more sentences describing your own room. Make sure to use adjectives that express the right meaning and feeling about your subject.

Forms of Adjectives 1

Adjectives have three forms: **positive, comparative,** and **superlative.** See the examples below. (Also refer to "Forms of Adjectives" on page 429 in the handbook.)

[Examples]

Positive: The high heels make me **tall**.
This game is **difficult**.

Comparative: The high heels make me **taller** than Maria.
This game is **more difficult** than the first one.

Superlative: The high heels make me the **tallest** girl in our class.
This is the **most difficult** game we've ever played.

Write three sentences for each of the following adjectives: *small*, *beautiful,* and *hungry*. Use the positive form of the adjective in the first sentence, the comparative form in the second sentence, and the superlative form in the third.

small

Positive: _____

_____

Comparative: _____

_____

Superlative: _____

_____

beautiful

Positive: _____

_____

Comparative: _____

_____

Superlative: _____

_____

hungry

Positive: _____

_____

Comparative: _____

_____

Superlative: _____

_____

Next Step

Write the comparative and superlative forms of these adjectives: *loud, smart, colorful.*

Forms of Adjectives 2

For some adjectives, such as *good* and *bad*, a completely different word is used to make the comparative and the superlative forms. Study the "Special Forms" chart on page 429 in the handbook to learn about these adjectives. Afterward, read the example sentences below. Pay close attention to the highlighted adjectives.

[Examples]   Puerto Rico's winters are **better** than New York's.
Puerto Rico has the **best** weather in the world.
Winter is the **worst** time in New York.
Too **many** cold days and too **little** sunshine make me sick.

Write three sentences like the ones above, comparing two places you have lived or visited. Use as many special forms of adjectives as you can. When you finish, underline all the special forms of adjectives. Exchange your sentences with a partner. Check each other's adjectives to make sure they are correctly stated.

_____

_____

_____

_____

Next Step

On a sheet of paper, write the heading "Special Forms of Adjectives." Under the heading, make columns labeled "Positive," "Comparative," and "Superlative." Now look at the sentences that you wrote above. Write each underlined adjective in the correct column. Then see if you can fill in the rest of your chart. Open your handbook to page 429 to check your work.

Using Colorful Adjectives

Colorful adjectives can make the nouns in your writing clearer and more interesting. Don't settle for the first adjective that comes to mind. It may be overused or uninteresting. (Refer to "Choosing Effective Modifiers" on page 111 in the handbook for guidelines and examples.)

 **Write two colorful adjectives that could be used instead of the underlined adjective in each sentence. (Use a thesaurus if you need help.) The first one has been done for you.**

1. Aki has some <u>pretty</u> fish called koi.

   _____ elegant _____   _____ colorful _____

2. They live in a <u>small</u> pond in the garden.

   _____   _____

3. Once a <u>big</u> raccoon ate two of Aki's koi.

   _____   _____

4. Aki was <u>mad</u>.

   _____   _____

5. Now when the raccoon comes, Aki makes <u>loud</u> noises to scare it away.

   _____   _____

6. But the <u>silly</u> raccoon keeps coming back, hoping for another fish dinner.

   _____   _____

Using Adverbs

Adverbs are used to modify verbs, adjectives, or other adverbs. There are four basic types of adverbs: *adverbs of time, place, manner,* and *degree.* (Refer to "Adverbs" on page 430 in the handbook for more information.)

Try It Out

In the chart below, arrange the list of adverbs according to the four different types. There are five adverbs per category. (Two of the words have been "charted" for you.)

yesterday	quite	calmly	ahead	now
nearby	carelessly	weekly	tightly	slightly
rapidly	backward	yonder	rather	anywhere
too	never	barely	after	smoothly

Time (when)	Place (where)	Manner (how)	Degree (to what extent)
yesterday	nearby		

Now add several more adverbs to each category. Discuss your results.

Write one sentence for each type of adverb listed below. (Use the adverbs from the chart on the previous page for your sentences.)

adverb of time

_____

_____

adverb of place

_____

_____

adverb of manner

_____

_____

adverb of degree

_____

_____

Next Step

Get creative with adverbs by writing at least one Tom Swifty. Two examples follow:

"Move faster," the boss said <u>rapidly</u>.

"Feel that air," my dad said <u>breezily</u>.

In each example, the underlined adverb reflects the other words in the sentence.

Forms of Adverbs

Adverbs have comparative and superlative forms. Refer to the example sentences below. (Also refer to "Forms of Adverbs" on page 431 in the handbook for more examples.)

[Examples]   The adverbs are underlined in each example sentence.

Troy reads <u>carefully</u>. (positive)

Troy reads <u>more carefully</u> than his friend. (comparative)

Troy reads the <u>most carefully</u> before an exam. (superlative)

Rewrite each sentence below two times. In your first sentence, use the comparative form of the underlined adverb. In your second sentence, use the superlative form of the adverb. The first one has been done for you.

1. Traymane sleeps <u>late</u>.

Traymane sleeps <u>later</u> than his brother.

Of all the days in the week, Traymane sleeps the <u>latest</u> on Saturdays.

2. Zong hits a baseball <u>hard</u>.

_____

_____

3. Carmela eats <u>slowly</u>.

_____

_____

4. Gloria cleans her room <u>quickly</u>.

_____

_____

Prepositions

Prepositions are words that show position or direction. Prepositions also introduce prepositional phrases. (Refer to "Prepositions" on page 432 in the handbook for a list of common prepositions.)

Practice   Underline the prepositions in the following sentences. (The number of prepositions in each sentence is indicated in parentheses.) The first sentence has been done for you.

1. There are hundreds of sunken ships below the oceans and seas of the world. (3)

2. In 1622, the *Atocha* sailed from Havana, Cuba, toward Spain. (3)

3. The ship was filled with treasure for the Spanish king; however, the treasure never made it across the Atlantic. (3)

4. Only two days into the voyage, the *Atocha* was hit by a hurricane. (2)

5. The ship was smashed upon a coral reef and sank beneath the waves. (2)

6. Everyone aboard the *Atocha* drowned except five lucky people. (2)

7. After 350 years, divers found the wreck of the *Atocha* on the ocean floor. (3)

8. Divers found gold and silver in and around the ship, along with other treasures. (3)

9. Everyone knows about the *Titanic*, which went down off the coast of Canada with more than 2,200 people aboard. (4)

10. The ship sank in water so deep that it wasn't found until 1985. (2)

11. Valuable objects have been found throughout the ship. (1)

12. No one is allowed to take anything from the wreck, though. (1)

13. It has been declared a memorial to the people who died when the *Titanic* slammed into an iceberg. (2)

Prepositional Phrases 1

A **prepositional phrase** includes a preposition, the object of the preposition (a noun or a pronoun), and any words that modify the object. Prepositional phrases are used to modify another part of the sentence. (Refer to "Prepositions" on page 432 in the handbook for more information.)

[Examples]   The parts of the following prepositional phrases are labeled:

down - the - dark - street
preposition adjective   adjective   noun object

over - the - long - bridge
preposition adjective   adjective   noun object

with - very - little - time
preposition   adverb   adjective   noun object

under - it
preposition   pronoun object

Try It Out

Find the list of prepositions in your handbook and then write three prepositional phrases of your own. Label the words in your phrases.

1. _____

_____

2. _____

_____

3. _____

_____

Share your work with a classmate.

Use each of your prepositional phrases in a sentence. (Use the space below for your work.) Note the sample sentence that follows.

The police officer chased the man <u>down the dark street</u>.

1. _____

_____

2. _____

_____

3. _____

_____

Change the preposition as many times as possible in the sample sentence. One new sentence has been done for you. *Note:* Some prepositions such as "along with" consist of two words. (Continue this exercise on your own paper.)

Sammy Smith walked <u>toward the other children</u>.

<u>Sammy Smith walked with the other children.</u>

_____

_____

_____

_____

Next Step

Exchange your work with a classmate and see who was able to use the most prepositions. (Refer to your handbook if you need help checking your partner's work.)

Prepositional Phrases 2

A **prepositional phrase** is a group of words beginning with a preposition such as *for, in, into, near,* etc. (Refer to "Prepositions" on page 432 in the handbook for a complete list.)

A prepositional phrase includes the preposition, the object of the preposition, and all the modifiers of the object. Here is an example:

by - **one** - **arm**
preposition   adjective   noun object

Note: A prepositional phrase may be used as an adjective or an adverb.

[**Examples**]   **The monkey <u>with the reddish fur</u> entertained us.**

The prepositional phrase *with the reddish fur* is an adjective. It tells *which* monkey.

Seven monkeys <u>live in the zoo</u>.

The prepositional phrase *in the zoo* is an adverb. It tells *where* the monkeys live.

Try It Out

Underline the prepositional phrase in this sentence.

Cleo saw a spider in the barn.

Fill in the blocks with the parts of the underlined phrase.

preposition	adjective	noun object

Is the prepositional phrase an adjective or an adverb? What does the phrase refer to or tell more about?

Study the prepositional phrase written in the blocks below. Then write two of your own prepositional phrases in the empty blocks and label the words.

up	the	stairs
preposition	adjective	noun object

1.

| | | |

_____   _____   _____

2.

| | | |

_____   _____   _____

Use your two prepositional phrases in sentences.

1. _____

_____

_____

2. _____

_____

_____

Using Interjections

An **interjection** is a word or words expressing strong emotion or surprise. Interjections are often used when writing dialogue for a story or play. An interjection is separated from the rest of a sentence by an exclamation mark or a comma.

[Examples] The interjections are underlined in the following examples:

<u>Wow</u>! Do you hear that humming sound?

<u>Hmm</u>, sounds like a swarm of bees.

Practice

Underline each interjection in the sentences below. Write your own interjection when a space is provided. The first two have been done for you.

1. "<u>Quick</u>! Close the window!" Lea yelled to Joe.

2. "<u>Yikes</u>, what's out there?"

3. "Wow, there's a big nest of hornets out there!"

4. "Joe, help me fix this window. Ouch! They're already getting in."

5. "Goodness," said their mom, "I wondered what the noise was all about."

6. "_____ , Mom, we're under attack!"

7. "Nonsense, hornets are harmless," said their mom.

8. "Really! Tell that to the one that just stung me!" cried Lea.

9. "Ow! One just got me!" yelled Joe.

10. "Well, I guess I'm confusing hornets with bees," said Mom.

11. "_____ , what a time for the phone to ring!" exclaimed Lea.

Practice

Write a phone conversation on the lines below. Include at least three interjections. Work on this section with a partner if your teacher allows it.

_____

_____

_____

_____

_____

_____

_____

_____

_____

_____

_____

_____

_____

_____

_____

_____

Next Step

Exchange conversations. Note how your classmates used and punctuated interjections in their work.

Coordinating Conjunctions

Coordinating conjunctions connect equal parts: two or more words, phrases, or clauses. (Refer to "Conjunctions" on page 433 in your handbook for more information.)

Use one of the coordinating conjunctions given in the box below to fill in each blank in the sentences that follow. The answers will vary.

and	but	or	so	yet

1. My parents said I could get a cat _____ a bird.

2. I like birds, _____ the neighbors gave me a kitten.

3. He was just a ball of fur, _____ I called him Chubbs.

4. Now my cat Chubbs is fat _____ lazy.

5. He sleeps on the couch _____ under my bed.

6. Chubbs hates exercise, _____ he stays fat.

7. He's friendly _____ independent.

8. Chubbs curls up beside me _____ not on my lap.

9. He likes to have his belly rubbed _____ his chin scratched.

10. My cat loves peanut butter, _____ it makes him sick.

11. Chubbs likes to sleep a lot, _____ he can be as playful as a kitten.

Coordinating conjunctions can be used to connect two simple sentences (or clauses) to create a compound sentence. (See pages 76 and 406 in your handbook for information on compound sentences.) Use a comma, plus the coordinating conjunction in the parentheses, to connect each pair of simple sentences below.

1. Angela made brownies. She gave me one. **(and)**

_____

2. Mateo wants to watch TV. He has homework to do first. **(but)**

_____

3. Yoshi did his homework already. He has a piano lesson later. **(for)**

_____

4. Caris lives nearby. He walks to school. **(so)**

_____

5. Tyrelle entered an art contest. He won first prize. **(and)**

_____

6. Garon has the flu. He is staying home from school. **(so)**

_____

7. Aldwin shares a room with Garon. Aldwin isn't sick. **(yet)**

_____

8. I called Isabel. She wasn't home. **(but)**

_____

9. Wake up your brother. He'll be late for school. **(or)**

_____

Coordinating and Correlative Conjunctions

Coordinating and **correlative conjunctions** connect equal parts: two or more words, phrases, or clauses. The handbook lists the different coordinating and correlative conjunctions. (Refer to "Kinds of Conjunctions" on page 433 in the handbook for this information.)

Rewrite each set of sentences below, following the guidelines in parentheses. The first one has been done for you.

1. John played on the varsity team. Bill played on the varsity team.
   (Use a coordinating conjunction to form a simple sentence with a compound subject.)

   John and Bill played on the varsity team.

2. Marius will pass the test. He will not get his license.
   (Use a comma and a correlative conjunction to form a compound sentence.)

   _____

3. Their team was small. Their team was fast.
   (Use a coordinating conjunction to join two adjectives in a simple sentence.)

   _____

4. Oki wanted to play. She sprained her ankle.
   (Use a comma and a coordinating conjunction to form a compound sentence.)

   _____

5. Paulo ran down the street. He ran across the bridge.
   (Use a coordinating conjunction to join two prepositional phrases in a simple sentence.)

   _____

6. Thea was not happy. Thea was not sad.
   (Use a correlative conjunction to join two adjectives in a simple sentence.)

   _____

7. The children laughed during recess. The children ran during recess.
(Use a coordinating conjunction to form a compound predicate, or verb, in a simple sentence.)

_____

8. Mohan can't come. Vishnu can't come.
(Use a correlative conjunction to form a compound subject in a simple sentence.)

_____

_____

9. Channa was sick. She stayed home from school.
(Use a comma and a coordinating conjunction to form a compound sentence.)

_____

10. Bonita went to Tanya's birthday party. Mara went to Tanya's birthday party.
(Use a correlative conjunction to join two subjects in a simple sentence.)

_____

Next Step

Write two sentences of your own. Use a different correlative conjunction in each of your sentences. Then exchange your work with a classmate and check each other's work.

Subordinating Conjunctions 1

Subordinating conjunctions connect two clauses to form a complex sentence. (Refer to "Kinds of Conjunctions" on page 433 in the handbook for more information.)

 **Underline the subordinating conjunction in each sentence below. The first sentence has been done for you.**

1. I have math class <u>after</u> I go to lunch.

2. I usually have time to go outside because I eat fast.

3. Most days we play basketball on the school grounds, although today it was raining.

4. I went to the library, where I got some books for my report.

5. When my report is done, I'm going to read a novel.

6. I want to read *Jesse* by Gary Soto because it is about a guy like me.

7. I won't have time for extra reading while I'm working on the report.

8. I can start the book this weekend if I finish my report by Friday.

9. My sister will help me do chores so that I can finish my research tonight.

10. If I have time, I want to read one more novel.

11. I won't decide what to read next until I finish *Jesse*.

12. I enjoy stories that make me feel as though I know the characters as friends.

Subordinating Conjunctions 2

Subordinating conjunctions connect two clauses to form a complex sentence. (Refer to "Kinds of Conjunctions" on page 433 in the handbook for more information.)

Practice

Choose subordinating conjunctions from the list in the box below and write them on the lines to complete the story. You may use them more than once.

after	before	so that	when
although	if	though	where
as if	in order that	unless	whereas
because	since	until	while

1   _____ I ate breakfast, I called Renaldo.

2   "I knew you'd forget your report _____ I called you," I said.

3   "I put it in my folder _____ I wouldn't forget it," Renaldo said.

4   _____ we met at the bus stop, he gave me a "thumbs up." He

5   thought he had the report _____ we were on the bus.

6   "It's gone!" he yelled. "I know I put it _____ it belonged!"

7   "_____ you panic, check your backpack," I said. I watched

8   _____ Renaldo searched frantically.

9   He calmed down _____ he saw his mom outside the school,

10   _____ his report was in her hand.

11   "It probably fell out of your folder _____ you left home," she said.

Next Step

Write your own school-related story. Use subordinating conjunctions to make at least three complex sentences.

Conjunctions Review

Conjunctions are words that connect other words, phrases, and clauses. Conjunctions help your writing move smoothly from one idea to the next. There are three main types of conjunctions: *coordinating, correlative,* and *subordinating.* (Refer to "Conjunctions" on page 433 in the handbook for more information and examples.)

[**Examples**] The conjunctions are highlighted in each of the following examples:

Guerdy finished her homework **before** she watched any TV.
(The subordinating conjunction *before* connects two clauses.)

David **and** Hopeton enjoy the same TV shows.
(The coordinating conjunction *and* connects two words.)

My money is **either** in my coat **or** on my dresser.
(The correlative conjunctions *either, or* connect two phrases.)

Combine each pair of sentences using a conjunction. Try to use a different conjunction in each of your new sentences. The first two have been done for you. (Answers will vary.)

1. Marsha enjoys many sports. Her sister hates any kind of exercise.

Marsha enjoys many sports, but her sister hates any kind of exercise.

_____

2. I sprained my ankle very badly. I didn't make the tennis team.

Because I sprained my ankle very badly, I didn't make the

tennis team.

(Subordinating conjunctions can be used at the beginning of sentences.)

3. Robert took the test four times. He finally raised his grade.

_____

_____

4. Bill was late for the game. John started in his place.

_____

_____

5. Mr. Evans is a good coach. His teams don't win many games.

_____

_____

6. My friend Johan has gained nearly 20 pounds. He won't stop eating.

_____

_____

7. Go to bed early tonight. You'll be too tired to play tomorrow.

_____

_____

8. I read the directions twice. I still didn't understand them.

_____

_____

Next Step

Exchange papers with a classmate and compare your partner's use of conjunctions with your own.

Parts of Speech Review

In the English language there are eight **parts of speech** (nouns, verbs, adjectives, etc.). They help you understand words and how to use them in sentences. The following activity reviews all eight parts of speech. (Refer to "Parts of Speech" in the handbook for more information.)

Try It Out

Each circle contains a list of words representing one of the eight parts of speech. Write the correct part of speech for each list of words on the blank in each circle. Discuss your answers with your classmates.

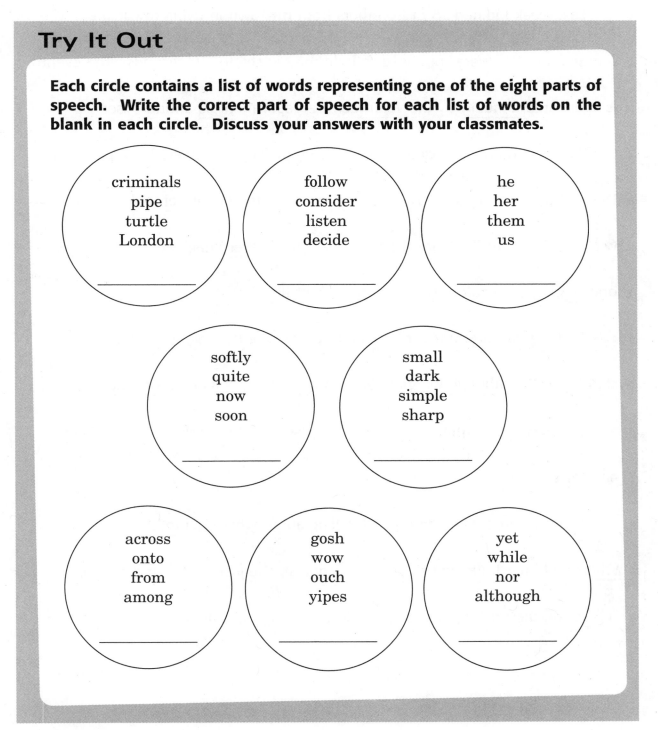

criminals
pipe
turtle
London
_____

follow
consider
listen
decide
_____

he
her
them
us
_____

softly
quite
now
soon
_____

small
dark
simple
sharp
_____

across
onto
from
among
_____

gosh
wow
ouch
yipes
_____

yet
while
nor
although
_____

Identify the part of speech for each underlined word. There are four examples of each part of speech, except for the interjection, which has one example. The first two have been done for you.

1   verb   preposition
     Last week I <u>joined</u> 15 or 20 others <u>from</u> my town in trying to catch a

2   greased pig. We were supposed to hold the pig still for 10 seconds. The event

3   is sponsored <u>annually</u> by the <u>volunteer</u> fire department <u>as</u> a fund-raiser.

4   The <u>local</u> humane society said the event posed no danger <u>to</u> the pig. <u>Boy</u>!

5   Did that prove to be true! Any danger, including the danger <u>of</u> looking foolish,

6   <u>was reserved</u> <u>specifically</u> for the humans. I had <u>never</u> imagined the <u>problems</u>

7   one <u>slippery</u> pig could create in such a <u>short</u> <u>time</u>.

8   That pig had the moves of a <u>halfback</u>. <u>It</u> made us look <u>as if</u> <u>we</u> were

9   standing still. <u>Although</u> we grabbed <u>frantically</u>, the pig always <u>escaped</u>.

10   Neither tackling nor tripping worked. We just ended up with grease <u>and</u> grass

11   all over us.

12   Walking home, <u>I</u> couldn't help thinking about what my <u>mother</u> had said.

13   <u>When</u> I told her I planned to enter the contest, <u>she</u> just smiled and added,

14   "I'll <u>bet</u> on the pig." I guess she knew something I didn't.

Minilessons

The minilessons in this section of your SkillsBook cover basic editing and proofreading skills. All the minilessons are cross-referenced with your handbook.

Marking Punctuation

The End . . . . Periods

READ about using periods on page 345 in your handbook.

Using one of your textbooks, **FIND** an example of each way to use a period: to end a sentence, after an initial, after an abbreviation, and as a decimal. If you can't find all four examples in one book, try a second book.

COPY the examples onto your own paper. (If the example is part of a sentence, copy the whole sentence.) Your teacher may want to categorize and label all the examples on a punctuation poster.

Keeping It Short . . . . Abbreviations

STUDY the table "Common Abbreviations" on page 370 with a partner.

On your own, **WRITE** down any five of the words and phrases, without their abbreviations, listed in the table.

TRADE papers. Without looking at the handbook, write the correct abbreviation next to each word or phrase your partner wrote down.

CHECK your abbreviations in the handbook.

DO this same activity again, writing down five different words or phrases. Trade papers.

Asking and Telling . . . . Question Marks

READ about using question marks on page 346 in your handbook.

TURN to page 339. **READ** about Ellen Ochoa. **IMAGINE** that you are going to interview her. On a sheet of paper, **WRITE** two direct questions that you'd like to ask Ellen Ochoa.

Then **WRITE** two indirect questions, telling a friend what you'd like to ask Ms. Ochoa.

USE the correct end punctuation for all four sentences.

Unbelievable! . . . . Exclamation Points

READ about using exclamation points on page 346 in your handbook.

IMAGINE that early this morning you saw an alien spaceship land.

You watched as two aliens got out, captured your neighbor's cat, and took him away in their ship. You were the only witness! Now you are being interviewed by a TV news reporter. **WRITE** down what you would say to the reporter. Use exclamation points in three different ways: after a word, after a phrase, and after a sentence.

This, That, These, and Those . . . . Commas in a Series

READ about using commas to separate items in a series on page 347 in your handbook.

WRITE a sentence that lists some of your favorite foods. **USE** commas correctly.

How many miles? .... Commas in Numbers

READ about using commas to keep numbers clear on page 347 in your handbook. **TURN** to page 447. **COPY** the numbers from the bottom row of the table. (You and a partner each copy the numbers.) Then take turns **READING** the numbers aloud. Here is the first one: "Eight hundred sixty-five thousand four hundred."

Putting It All Together .... Commas in Compound Sentences

READ about using commas in compound sentences on page 350 in your handbook. You can see more examples of commas in compound sentences on pages 76 and 406.

TURN to page 328. **FIND** the two compound sentences in "A Very Special Day." Copy them onto a sheet of paper. Draw a circle around the comma that is before the connecting word in each sentence.

Next, **FIND** two sentences in "A Very Special Day" that can be combined to make a compound sentence. (Remember to use *and, but, or, nor, for, so,* or *yet.*) **WRITE** the compound sentence and put a comma where it is needed.

FIND two more sentences that can be combined. Write the compound sentence.

In the Beginning .... Commas with Introductory Phrases and Clauses

On page 350 in your handbook, **READ** about using commas to separate introductory phrases and clauses.

TURN to page 80 in your handbook. **FIND** the introductory phrases and clauses in the sample paragraph. (*Hint:* There are five of them.)

COPY these phrases and clauses, putting a comma and a few of the follow-up words after each. (*Example: On his head, a knight wore . . .*)

2 = 1 .... Semicolons

READ about using semicolons to join two independent clauses on page 353 in your handbook. Then **TURN** to page 266.

REWRITE the first two sentences of the model labeled "Study-Reading." Use a semicolon to turn these two sentences into one sentence. Now combine the last two sentences.

Either way, it works. .... Colons and Commas

READ about using a colon to introduce a list on page 354 in your handbook.

MAKE a list of at least five things you use at school each day.

WRITE a sentence using this list. In this sentence, use a colon. Write another sentence using the same list. In the second sentence, use only commas, no colon. (See handbook page 347.)

Great Connections .... Hyphens

READ about using hyphens with *self, ex, all,* and *great* on page 356 in your handbook. The prefix *great* means "one generation older or younger." For example, your great-grandmother is one generation older than your grandmother.

WRITE as many family words as you can using *great*. (*Hint:* If you are your grandfather's grandson, what are you to your great-grandfather?) **USE** hyphens correctly.

"Hey, don't I know you?" .... Quotation Marks

READ about quotation marks on pages 357 and 358 in your handbook. Pay special attention to "To Set Off the Exact Words of a Speaker" and "Placement of Punctuation."

IMAGINE meeting your favorite TV star. **WRITE** a few sentences telling what you might say to each other. Use quotation marks correctly.

Name That Poem .... Quotation Marks

READ about using quotation marks to punctuate titles on page 357 in your handbook.

TURN to page 169. **READ** the poem by Gema Diaz. Then, **WRITE** a sentence telling the name of the poem and an opinion about it. **USE** quotation marks correctly.

   Example: I like the way the writer repeats words in "Everything Is New for Me."

READ the two poems on page 170. **WRITE** a sentence about each poem on page 170, telling its name and an opinion about it.

Kim's, Sue's, Juan's . . . . Singular Possessives

READ about using apostrophes to form singular possessives on 359 in your handbook.

LIST the first names of 10 people you know. Next to each name, **WRITE** the possessive form of the name, followed by something that belongs to each one.

Man/Men/Men's .... Plural Possessives

READ about using apostrophes to form plural possessives on the top of page 360 in your handbook. Then **WRITE** these words: *computer, snake, woman*. Next to each word, **WRITE** its plural form and the plural possessive form of the word.

Finally, **WRITE** three sentences using one of your plural possessive words in each one.

Extra! .... Parentheses

READ about parentheses on page 361 in your handbook. **TURN** to page 157 and find two examples of parentheses in the model.

FIND the parentheses (round a word, a phrase, or a complete sentence) in the models on pages 158 and 159, too.

CHOOSE a sentence from any one of these models. **ADD** something to the sentence, using parentheses. (Use your imagination!) Write your new sentence on your own paper.

Editing for Mechanics

Favorites .... Capitalization

OPEN your handbook to page 363. **READ** the section at the bottom of the page about capitalizing titles.

On a sheet of paper, **WRITE** the titles of your favorite movies, books, stories, poems, and songs. **WRITE** at least five titles all together. Use capital letters correctly.

World Citizens .... Capitalization

Do this minilesson with a partner.

READ page 365 in your handbook. **FILL IN** the blanks of the following sentence in as many different ways as you can. (Use the map section, pages 467-476, and the information on pages 436-437 of your handbook to help you with this activity.)

The _____ **people live in** _____ **and speak**
    (nationality)   (country)

_____.
    (language)

Some of your sentences may list more than one language.

The _____ **people live in** _____ **and speak**
    (nationality)   (country)

_____.
    (languages)

USE capital letters correctly. If you have time, use a dictionary or an atlas to check your spelling.

States and Sections .... Capitalization

OPEN your handbook to page 365. **READ** the section at the top of the page, "Particular Sections of the Country." Here are some commonly used names for sections of the country:

Northeast	**Midwest**	**West Coast**
South	**Great Plains**	

Now **TURN** to the U.S. map on page 469.

WRITE a sentence about each section of the country named above. Each sentence should name a few states that you think are in that section. Use the name of the section of the country in your sentence, too.

Example: Montana, Wyoming, and the Dakotas are part of the Great Plains.

Two of Everything .... Plural Nouns

Do this minilesson with a partner. **READ** the first section of page 367 in the
"Proofreader's Guide."

WRITE the example words you see there (*bicycle—bicycles, chair—chairs, brush—brushes,*
and so on). Leave some blank lines under each pair of words.

Under each pair of words, **WRITE** at least one more pair (singular and plural) that rhymes
with the example. The first one has been done for you.

- **bicycle - bicycles**
  tricycle - tricycles
  icicle - icicles

THINK of as many rhyming words as you can for the rest of the examples. (*Hint:* In your
mind, take off the beginning sound of the example word and try replacing it with
different sounds. *Chair* without the *ch* is *air.* Add *p,* and you have *pair.*)

How do you double an elf? .... Plurals

OPEN your handbook to page 368. **READ** "Nouns Ending in *f* or *fe.*"
COPY the 10 words below on a sheet of paper..

Then, next to each noun **WRITE** the plural form of the noun. Try saying the plural before
you write it. Remember, if the plural ends with a *v* sound, change the *f* to *ve* and add *s.*
(One of the words will be correct either way you make the plural. Can you guess
which word it is? Which word sounds right either way?)

calf	**dwarf**	**elf**	**gulf**	**half**
loaf	**puff**	**self**	**shelf**	**staff**

The "y" of Spelling .... Spelling

OPEN your handbook to page 368. **READ** "Nouns Ending in *y.*" Then close your handbook. On a sheet of paper, **COPY** the 10 words below.

Next to each word, **WRITE** the plural form of the word.

Then use your handbook to **CHECK** your work.

donkey	**fly**	**flurry**	**French fry**	**guppy**
monkey	**toy**	**puppy**	**turkey**	**pony**

Millions of Mice .... Numbers

READ page 371 in your handbook. **WRITE** a very short story that begins "Once upon a
time . . . ." **WRITE** about two brothers, ages 8 and 14, who had two pet mice. The
mouse family kept growing and growing until the brothers had millions of mice.
Include exactly how many mice you think the brothers had in the end. What did they
do with all those mice? (Use numerals or words for your numbers.)

Improving Your Spelling

Breaking the Rules .... Spelling

As you know, English spelling can be tricky. You must learn the rules as well as the exceptions to the rules. Without opening your handbook, try to **ANSWER** this question:

The words *either, weird, seize,* and *their* are exceptions to which spelling rule?

OPEN your handbook to page 378 to check your answer. Now **WRITE** some words that do follow the rule.

"I tried!" .... Spelling

STUDY the spelling rules "Silent *e*" and "Words Ending in *y*" on page 378 in your handbook.

Close your handbook. Then **WRITE** a sentence using the **past tense** of each of these verbs:

die	**dye**	**lie**	**tie**
dry	**fry**	**spy**	

Double Up .... Spelling

STUDY the spelling rules for "Words Ending in a Consonant" on page 378 in your handbook.

Close your handbook. Then add *ing* to the following words. **WRITE** your words on a separate sheet of paper. The first two have been done for you.

bloom _blooming_		**lead** _____	
brag _bragging_		**begin** _____	
tag _____		**control** _____	
plan _____		**wag** _____	
help _____		**sag** _____	
occur _____		**hug** _____	
answer _____		**permit** _____	
remember _____		**shed** _____	
map _____		**drag** _____	
develop _____		**walk** _____	
scream _____		**appeal** _____	

Commonly Misused Words

Accepting the Challenge! .... Commonly Misused Words

STUDY the commonly misused words on page 379 in your handbook.
USE each of the words *a, an, accept, except, allowed,* and *aloud* correctly in a sentence.
LOOK back at page 379 if you need to review how to use the words correctly.

> **Examples:** I'd like *an* omelette for breakfast.
>
> I'll have *a* glass of juice, too.

Spelling makes the difference. .... Commonly Misused Words

Do this minilesson with a partner. **OPEN** your handbook to page 381. Together, study the word pair *blew* and *blue*.

On your own, **WRITE** one sentence using *blew* or *blue* correctly.

READ your sentence to your partner, and have your partner **WRITE** down *blue* or *blew*, correctly spelling the word you used in your sentence.

Then **LISTEN** as your partner reads his or her sentence. **WRITE** down *blue* or *blew*, whichever is used in the sentence.

CHECK each other's work.

You can also do this minilesson with these word pairs:

desert, dessert (page 383)	**plain, plane** (page 389)
flower, flour (page 384)	**tail, tale** (page 392)
hear, here (page 385)	**wait, weight** (page 393)
meat, meet (page 387)	

For a challenge, try writing sentences that use both words of a pair.

Bring and Take .... Commonly Misused Words

OPEN your handbook to page 381. **READ** about the word pair *bring* and *take*.

TURN to page 175 and **READ** about "alliteration." Then **WRITE** a sentence for each word using as much alliteration as you can.

> **Examples:** Bring me both boxes of bananas.
>
> Take these two telephones to Tomas.

Try this exercise with other word pairs.

It's licking its lips! .... Commonly Misused Words

OPEN your handbook to page 385. **STUDY** the word pair *its* and *it's*.

WRITE a short paragraph about a visitor from outer space. Your paragraph should describe what the space creature looks like and what it is doing. Use both *its* and *it's* at least twice.

Here is a sample beginning:

The space creature looks like a big yellow lizard walking on its back legs. It's looking at my lunch as if it's hungry.

Lead On! .... Commonly Misused Words

OPEN your handbook to page 386. **READ** about the word pair *lead* and *led*.

Close your handbook and **WRITE** a sentence for each one of the following words. (Make sure to use each word correctly.)

    lead (meaning "to guide")

    led (meaning "guided"; past tense of *lead)*

    lead (the name of a metal)

READ your sentences aloud for a classmate, pronouncing *lead, led,* and *lead* correctly.

Match Madness .... Commonly Misused Words

Without looking in your handbook, try to **MATCH** each word below with the correct definition. The first one has been done for you. When you are finished, **CHECK** and **CORRECT** your answers by looking over handbook pages 380-381.

1. ate ___g___   a. piece of wood
2. eight _____   b. without covering
3. bare _____   c. to purchase
4. bear _____   d. tired of something
5. by _____   e. near
6. buy _____   f. large, furry animal
7. board _____   g. to have eaten
8. bored _____   h. the number 8

Brain Buster .... Commonly Misused Words

Here's a special challenge. **CHOOSE** a pair of words from pages 379-394 in your handbook. Show that you understand how to use the words correctly by **WRITING** an appropriate acrostic poem for each. See handbook page 177 and the example poems below for help.

SEA / SEE

    Seals play   **S**o happy to look at

    Each day   **E**verything,

    Among the waves.   **E**verywhere.

Understanding Idioms

Sink or swim. .... Idioms

Do this minilesson with a partner. **OPEN** your handbook to page 400.
READ about each idiom. Then **MAKE UP** your own sentences using the idioms correctly.
Your sentences can be about yourself, your partner, or people you know. And you don't
    need to write them down; just say them aloud to your partner.
MAKE UP sentences for at least five of the idioms on page 400.

Saying What You Mean .... Idioms

Do this minilesson in a group of three to five students. **OPEN** your handbooks to pages
    395-401.
DISCUSS a few of the most interesting idioms you find there.
TALK about why you think each idiom means what it means. (For example, why would "as
    the crow flies" mean "in a straight line"?) Some will be easy to figure out; others will
    be a mystery! Does anyone in the group know an idiom in a different language that
    means the same thing? An English speaker who said something embarrassing would
    say, "I put my foot in my mouth." But a French speaker would say, "I put my finger in
    my eye."

Shake a leg. .... Idioms

Do this minilesson with a partner. **OPEN** your handbook to pages 395-401. **CHOOSE** one
    page. Act out (pantomime) one idiom. Your partner guesses which one it is and then
    uses that idiom in a sentence. **CHOOSE** another page. Now your partner acts out an
    idiom. **GUESS** which one it is and then use it in a sentence. Continue taking turns.

Picture this. .... Idioms

Open your handbook to page 401. **CHOOSE** any idiom on this page and **DRAW** a cartoon
    to illustrate it. For example, if you chose "sweet tooth," you could draw a picture of
    yourself with candy bars for teeth.
After you draw your cartoon, **WRITE** a caption for it. (A caption is a sentence that is
    written under a cartoon to explain it.) **USE** your idiom in your caption.
    Example: "I have a sweet tooth!"

Understanding Sentences

First, the Basics .... Parts of a Sentence

Do this minilesson with a partner. **READ** about "Parts of a Sentence" on page 402 in your handbook. (You also may want to review "Basic Parts of a Sentence" on page 66.)

TURN to page 430. **READ** the five sentences at the top of the page.

Together, **FIND** the simple subject and predicate (verb) in each sentence. You don't need to write them down; just say them aloud.

Do this now! .... Parts of a Sentence

READ about "Parts of a Sentence" on page 402 in your handbook. Pay special attention to the examples of an understood subject and an understood predicate.

WRITE one sentence of your own that has an understood subject.

Then **WRITE** a question and an answer. Use an understood predicate in your answer.

Compound Underground .... Subjects and Predicates

STUDY page 403 in your handbook. Pay special attention to the section about compound predicates.

Now **TURN** to page 190. As you **READ** "Train Number Seven," look for the sentence that has a compound predicate. (There is only one!)

COPY the sentence and underline the compound predicate.

CIRCLE the subject of the sentence.

It takes two. .... Clauses

STUDY clauses on page 404 in your handbook. Pay special attention to the section about dependent clauses. Make sure you understand what a complex sentence is (page 406).

TURN to page 94 and **FIND** the five complex sentences in the essay (one in each paragraph).

COPY the dependent clause in each complex sentence on your own paper. The dependent clause may be at the beginning of the sentence or at the end. All the dependent clauses begin with subordinating conjunctions. (You will find a list of these on page 433.)

CIRCLE the subordinating conjunction in each dependent clause.

One of Each .... Types of Sentences

READ about the three types of sentences on page 406 in your handbook.
Then **TURN** to page 196 and find one of each type of sentence in the sample report—a
    simple sentence, a compound sentence, and a complex sentence.
COPY the sentences and label each one.

Who wrote that? I did! .... Kinds of Sentences

READ about the four kinds of sentences on page 407 in your handbook.
Then **TURN** to page 139 and find one of each kind of sentence in the sample letter.
COPY the sentences and **LABEL** each one.

Tag Alongs .... Kinds of Sentences

READ about tag questions on page 407 in your handbook.
Then add tag questions to the following sentences.

That was the final runner, _____?

This wasn't his first game, _____?

It's your birthday today, _____?

Geoff isn't your brother, _____?

WRITE at least one tag-question sentence of your own.

The Parts of Speech

Abstract Nouns . . . . Nouns

READ about concrete nouns and abstract nouns on page 409 in your handbook.

Then **TURN** to page 90. **LIST** all the abstract nouns you find in the sample information essay. (Many of the nouns appear more than once, but you only need to write them one time.)

The flock stops here. . . . . Collective Nouns

Do this minilesson with a partner. **READ** about collective nouns on the bottom of page 410 in your handbook.

Then **TURN** to page 441 and **LOOK** at the table of animal facts. The words in the group column are all collective nouns.

Take turns **MAKING UP** funny sentences using these words. You don't need to write your sentences—just say them aloud to your partner. *Note:* Collective nouns often take singular verbs.

Examples: A sleuth of bears is asleep on the sofa.

A clutter of cats has too many claws.

Note: See *A Cache of Jewels and Other Collective Nouns* by Ruth Heller.

Uncountable . . . . Count and Noncount Nouns

Do this minilesson with a partner. **READ** about count and noncount nouns on page 411 in your handbook. Pay special attention to the section "Noncount Nouns." Take turns **MAKING UP** sentences using the example words (*sugar, furniture, luck, happiness*).
SAY your sentences aloud.

Now **MAKE UP** sentences using the example words that can be either count or noncount nouns (*hair, light, paper, chicken*). Use each word both ways.

Example: I see *light* coming from under the door. (noncount)

Please turn on a *light* so I can see. (count)

Whose dreams? .... Pronouns and Antecedents

READ about pronouns on page 413 in your handbook. Pay special attention to the section about personal pronouns.

TURN to page 148 and **READ** "The Power of the Dream." Look for the personal pronouns. On a sheet of paper, **LIST** these particular ones: *we, our, I, her, she, my, them.*

Next to each personal pronoun, **WRITE** its noun antecedent. The first one has been done for you.

   ■ **we — Chirayu and his class**

Extra Challenge: The personal pronoun *they* also appears in the sample. It has different antecedents in different sentences. Each time you find *they*, figure out what its antecedent is in the sentence. (*Note:* For this minilesson, read the sample essay only, not the side notes.)

Pizza, anyone? .... Pronouns

READ about interrogative pronouns on page 416 in your handbook.

WRITE four sentences about pizza. **BEGIN** each sentence with one of these interrogative pronouns: *who, whose, which, what.*

NOTICE that sentences that begin with interrogative pronouns are interrogative sentences. (See page 407 for an explanation of interrogative sentences.)

Can you do this? .... Modal Verbs

With a partner **STUDY** the table "Common Modal Verbs" on page 418 in your handbook.

Keep your handbook open to page 418 but have your partner close hers. **CHOOSE** any modal verb and say it aloud.

Have your partner **SAY** a sentence that uses the modal verb.

   Example: You say, "May."

   Your partner says, "I may have pizza for lunch."

Continue saying verbs for your partner for 2 or 3 minutes. Then **TRADE** places. Your partner will call out modal verbs, and you will say sentences using them.

Past, Present, and Future Values .... Verb Tenses

READ "Tenses of Verbs" on page 419 in your handbook.
TURN to page 90. In writing "My Personal Values," Eng Lee used past tense, present tense, and future tense verbs.
FIND and **COPY** one sentence that uses only present tense verbs. Underline the verbs. Label the sentence "present tense."
FIND and **COPY** one sentence that uses only future tense verbs. Underline the verbs. Label the sentence "future tense."
FIND and **COPY** one sentence that uses past, present, and future tense verbs. Underline the verbs. Label each verb to show what tense it is.

It happened last week. .... Verb Tenses

Do this lesson with a partner. **READ** "Tenses of Verbs" on page 419 in your handbook.
Then **TURN** to page 190 and read "Train Number Seven." Notice that all the verbs are in the present tense.
Now take turns **READING** the essay aloud, paragraph by paragraph. Imagine that you are the author, telling about a ride you took last week.
REREAD the first two paragraphs and **CHANGE** all the verbs to past tense. (*Note:* Do not change the sentences that appear in quotation marks.)

Don't just sit there! .... Active and Passive Verbs

READ about active and passive voice on page 421 in your handbook.
TURN to page 247 and read the sample paragraph. **FIND** the five sentences that have passive verbs. **COPY** the passive verbs onto your own paper. (All five passive verbs are phrases, not single words. The first one to appear in the paragraph has been given below.)
REWRITE two of the sentences in the active voice.

■ **is put**

One-of-a-Kind Verbs .... Irregular Verbs

Do this minilesson with a partner. **OPEN** your handbook to page 422. **CHOOSE** an irregular verb to practice.
Together, **MAKE UP** sentences using each of the three principal parts of the verb.
   Example: We begin doing math at noon.
             We began doing math at noon.
             We had begun doing math at noon.

You do not need to write your sentences—just say them aloud. Remember, always use *has, have,* or *had* with the past participle.

The End of Your Story .... Transitive Verbs

READ "Uses of Action Verbs" on page 424 in your handbook. Pay close attention to the first two sections.

On a sheet of paper, **COPY** these sentence beginnings:

- ■ **Ms. Mankiller helped**
- ■ **Wilma Mankiller won**
- ■ **She also received**
- ■ **Today Ms. Mankiller gives**

TURN to page 197 where you will find the information needed to complete these sentences. **WRITE** the necessary word or phrase after each beginning. You just added a direct object to each sentence. **CIRCLE** each direct object. (Remember, direct objects are usually nouns.) **UNDERLINE** each transitive verb.

That's all. .... Intransitive Verbs

READ about intransitive verbs on page 425 in your handbook.

On a sheet of paper, **LIST** the first names of five students in your class.

After each name, **WRITE** one word (a verb) to make a complete sentence.

> **Examples:** Tanya laughed.
>
> Misha frowned.

The verbs you will write are intransitive verbs; they do not need other words to complete their meaning.

Far, Faraway .... Adjectives

READ "Forms of Adjectives" on page 429 in your handbook. Don't forget to **STUDY** the "Special Forms of Adjectives" at the bottom of the page.

Then **TURN** to page 446. On a sheet of paper, **LIST** all the comparative and superlative adjectives you find.

WRITE a *c* for comparative or an *s* for superlative next to each adjective.

Daneesha sings best. .... Adverbs

READ about the forms of adverbs on page 431 in your handbook.

STUDY the "Special Forms" shown in the table.

CHOOSE one of the adverbs listed there (*well, badly, quickly,* or *fairly*).

WRITE three sentences, one using the positive form of the adverb, one using the comparative form, and one using the superlative form.

Poolside .... Prepositions

READ about prepositions on page 432 in your handbook.

IMAGINE that you and your friends are at a swimming pool.

WRITE five sentences about what is happening. **USE** at least one preposition in each sentence.

> **Examples:** Alisha jumped *off* the diving board.
>
> Erin swam *across* the pool.

Either it's raining or it's not! .... Conjunctions

READ about conjunctions on page 433 in your handbook. Pay special attention to the section on correlative conjunctions.

STUDY the list of correlative conjunctions in the table at the bottom of the page.

CHOOSE one pair of correlative conjunctions and use them in a sentence.

Wow! .... Interjections

REVIEW the interjections listed on page 349 in your handbook. **USE** each one of these words in a sentence, and **MAKE SURE** to include a comma or an exclamation point after each interjection. **READ** your sentences out loud to a classmate.

Daily Sentences

The Daily Sentences in this section of your SkillsBook come in two different varieties. The focused sentences help you concentrate on one proofreading skill at a time. The proofreading sentences provide two or three different types of errors for you to correct.

Focused Sentences

■ **End Punctuation**

Do you know when baseball began

■ **End Punctuation**

Baseball was first played in the United States in 1846

■ **End Punctuation**

Today, baseball is the most popular sport in many

countries

■ **End Punctuation**

Have you ever watched a major-league baseball game

■ **End Punctuation**

Wow, more than 120 million people attend major-league

baseball games in a season

Focused Sentences

■ **Commas (In a Series)**

A healthful diet includes foods from the dairy group bread group meat group and vegetable/fruit group.

■ **Commas (In a Series)**

Foods like pasta bagels and crackers belong to the bread group.

■ **Commas (In a Series)**

Food supplies our bodies with proteins carbohydrates fats vitamins and minerals.

■ **Commas (In a Series)**

Grapefruit lemons and oranges are good sources of vitamin C.

■ **Commas (In a Series)**

We should eat healthful foods exercise regularly and practice good sleeping habits.

Focused Sentences

■ **Commas (Between Independent Clauses)**

Russia is the country with the largest area but China is the country with the largest population.

■ **Commas (Between Independent Clauses)**

The Nile River is in Africa and the Amazon River is in South America.

■ **Commas (Between Independent Clauses)**

Australia is in the Southern Hemisphere and Europe is in the Northern Hemisphere.

■ **Commas (Between Independent Clauses)**

The Pacific Ocean covers one-third of the surface of the world but it does not come in contact with Africa or Europe.

■ **Commas (Between Independent Clauses)**

Mount Everest is the highest mountain in the world so serious mountain climbers want to conquer it.

Focused Sentences

■ **Commas (To Set Off Appositives)**

The giant swallowtail a huge black and white butterfly is found in Africa.

■ **Commas (To Set Off Appositives)**

One of the smallest butterflies the western pygmy blue lives in North America.

■ **Commas (To Set Off Appositives)**

One family of butterflies the skippers have hairy bodies.

■ **Commas (To Set Off Appositives)**

The monarch a member of the milkweed butterfly family is famous for its long flight south each fall.

■ **Commas (To Set Off Appositives)**

The ancient Greeks' symbol for the soul was Psyche a butterfly-winged girl.

Focused Sentences

■ **Commas (To Set Off Long Introductory Phrases and Clauses)**

To help locate valuable natural resources scientists study physical maps.

■ **Commas (To Set Off Long Introductory Phrases and Clauses)**

When you explore a new city use a street map as a guide.

■ **Commas (To Set Off Long Introductory Phrases and Clauses)**

While studying for a geography test we used three different maps.

■ **Commas (To Set Off Long Introductory Phrases and Clauses)**

To read almost any type of map you need to refer to the map's legend and scale.

■ **Commas (To Set Off Long Introductory Phrases and Clauses)**

If you draw a map for a friend make sure that you label everything very clearly.

Focused Sentences

■ **Semicolon**

People long ago had no system of money they traded different goods instead.

■ **Semicolon**

People have used beads, shells, and stones as money however, metal coins have been the most popular kind of money.

■ **Semicolon**

At one time, the Chinese used little bronze tools as money these tools led to the development of coins.

■ **Semicolon**

Large Spanish dollars could be chopped into eight pieces to make change thus, they were called pieces of eight.

■ **Semicolon**

The basic unit of money in the United States is the dollar a basic unit of money in Europe is the euro.

Focused Sentences

■ **Colon**

We studied the five senses sight, hearing, smell, taste, and touch.

■ **Colon**

Human taste buds can detect the following flavors sweet, sour, salty, and bitter.

■ **Colon**

These are some of my favorite smells pizza, just-baked brownies, and anything with cinnamon.

■ **Colon**

To expand their sense of sight, people use these tools microscopes, telescopes, and binoculars.

■ **Colon**

Our skin contains receptors that allow us to feel these things touch, pain, heat, and cold.

Focused Sentences

■ **Apostrophes**

Abraham Lincolns birthplace is near Hodgenville, Kentucky.

■ **Apostrophes**

His wifes name was Mary Todd, and his childrens names were Edward, Willie, and Robert.

■ **Apostrophes**

Abraham Lincoln, Americas 16th president, faced the nations only civil war.

■ **Apostrophes**

His armys strength was its great number of soldiers; its weakness was the soldiers commanding generals.

■ **Apostrophes**

An assassins bullet tragically ended Lincolns life; he was only 56 years old when he died.

Focused Sentences

■ **Quotation Marks**

The Star-Spangled Banner is the official national anthem in the United States.

■ **Quotation Marks**

Dimitri said, They always sing the national anthem before baseball games.

■ **Quotation Marks**

I could never sing in front of a large group of people, said Ana.

■ **Quotation Marks**

One chapter in our history book is called Songs of Liberty.

■ **Quotation Marks**

Some people think that the song America is the United States' other national anthem.

Focused Sentences

■ **Italics (Underlining)**

The main characters in The Miracle Worker (a play) are Annie Sullivan and Helen Keller.

■ **Italics (Underlining)**

Have you read the book The Diary of Anne Frank?

■ **Italics (Underlining)**

Sports Illustrated is the most popular magazine in our library.

■ **Italics (Underlining)**

The Japanese word sayonara means "good-bye."

■ **Italics (Underlining)**

Apollo 11 astronauts landed the first spaceship on the moon.

Focused Sentences

■ **Capitalization**

the philippines is an island country in the pacific ocean.

■ **Capitalization**

The people of the philippines are called filipinos.

■ **Capitalization**

The philippines has more christians than does any other
country in asia.

■ **Capitalization**

In 1521, the spanish explorer ferdinand magellan arrived
in the philippines.

■ **Capitalization**

manuel roxas became the first president of the philippines;
manila became the first capital city.

Focused Sentences

■ **Plurals**

China has many large citys, including Shanghai, which has about nine million citizenes.

■ **Plurals**

In China, husbands and wifes are not allowed to have many childs.

■ **Plurals**

Most city people live in large apartment complexs; sometimes two familys share one apartment.

■ **Plurals**

Radioes, bicycles, and sewing machines are common in rural China; automobiles, television sets, and pianoes are not.

■ **Plurals**

Different kindes of fish are an important part of the Chinese diet; roasted sweet potatos are a popular treat.

Focused Sentences

■ **Numbers**

In eighteen seventy-six, Colorado became the thirty-eighth state.

■ **Numbers**

There are only 7 states in the country (two of which are Rocky Mountain states) that are larger in size than Colorado.

■ **Numbers**

The Denver Mint in Colorado can produce 40,000,000 coins a day.

■ **Numbers**

On average, Colorado gets fifteen inches of precipitation (rain and snow) a year.

■ **Numbers**

There are only forty-three people per square mile in Colorado; eighty-one people per square mile is the average for the United States.

Focused Sentences

■ **Using the Right Word**

In the United States, their are three branches of government, each with it's own duties and responsibilities.

■ **Using the Right Word**

The executive branch is headed buy the president, who appoints an cabinet to help him.

■ **Using the Right Word**

In the legislative branch, a large amount of bills are introduced, but only a few are past (changed into laws).

■ **Using the Right Word**

The judicial branch interprets each law, witch means that it reviews a law in an specific case to sea if it is valid.

■ **Using the Right Word**

One part of the Constitution gives Americans basic writes, including the freedom too worship and too speak openly.

Focused Sentences

■ **Combining Sentences (Series of Words)**

Argentina is a South American country. Brazil is also a South American country. Venezuela is one, too.

■ **Combining Sentences (Compound Sentence)**

Portuguese is the major language in Brazil. Spanish is the major language in Argentina.

■ **Combining Sentences (Appositive Phrase)**

Coffee is grown in the cool highlands. It is one of South America's most important crops.

■ **Combining Sentences (Prepositional Phrase)**

Sugar cane and bananas are important crops. They are important crops in the lowlands.

■ **Combining Sentences (Compound Verb)**

Latin Americans of today are a mixture of Europeans, Africans, and Indians. They have a rich and varied culture.

Focused Sentences

- **Subject-Verb Agreement**

   Of all of the animals, only birds has feathers.

- **Subject-Verb Agreement**

   The fastest bird fly over 100 miles per hour.

- **Subject-Verb Agreement**

   Either the ostrich or the penguin are a waterbird.

- **Subject-Verb Agreement**

   Ducks, gulls, and many other birds always lives

   near water.

- **Subject-Verb Agreement**

   One of the common songbirds are the canary.

Proofreading Sentences: Women Inventors 1

■ Using the Right Word, Plurals, Capitalization

Sara Josephine Baker became won of the first womans

to practice medicine in the united states.

■ Using the Right Word, Plurals

As an doctor, she treated the poorest childs in New York.

■ Punctuation (Period), Singular Possessive, Using the Right Word

One of Dr Bakers inventions was simple baby clothing,

designed too prevent accidental death by suffocation.

(Suffocate means "to choke or be smothered to death.")

■ Commas (To Set Off Interruptions), Using the Right Word, Run-On Sentence

In addition Dr. Baker invented a knew type of eyedrop for

babies it helped prevent blindness.

■ Commas (To Separate Introductory Phrases), Adjectives (Superlative), Capitalization

As a city health inspector Dr. Baker saw the most poorest

health conditions in New York city.

Proofreading Sentences: Women Inventors 2

■ **Subject-Verb Agreement, Commas (In Compound Sentences), Using the Right Word**

Grace Hopper were a great American computer expert and she served as an rear admiral in the U.S. Navy.

■ **Commas (To Set Off Appositives), Plural Possessive, Using the Right Word**

Dr. Hopper went to Vassar one of the top womens universities wear she studied math and physics.

■ **Commas (To Separate Introductory Phrases), Punctuation (Period), Irregular Verb (Past Tense)**

While in the navy Dr Hopper becomed the third person ever to program a large computer.

■ **Numbers, Commas (In a Series)**

The large computer was fifty-one feet long 8 feet high and 8 feet wide!

■ **Commas (To Separate Introductory Phrases), Double Subject, Adjectives (Comparative)**

By inventing a special computer language Dr. Hopper she made computing much more easier.

Proofreading Sentences: The Study of Life

■ **Subject-Verb Agreement, Sentence Fragment**

Plants and animals is living things. But not books and

bicycles.

■ **Commas (In a Series), Run-On Sentence, Pronoun-Antecedent Agreement, Subject-Verb Agreement**

Living things reproduce grow and develop it also needs food

and water.

■ **Subject-Verb Agreement, Contractions, End Punctuation**

Living things has many small cells, dont they

■ **Using the Right Word, Comma Splice**

As human beings, hour bodies need oxygen, green plants

produce it four us.

■ **Subject-Verb Agreement, Double Negative**

A plant have many cells and do not never move in the way

animals move.

Proofreading Sentences: The Plant Kingdom

■ **Using the Right Word, Sentence Fragment**

Plants make food. Buy photosynthesis.

■ **Commas (To Separate Introductory Phrases), Commas (In a Series), Using the Right Word**

In the process of photosynthesis plants use sunlight carbon dioxide and water too make food.

■ **Subject-Verb Agreement, End Punctuation**

Plants gives off oxygen during photosynthesis, don't they

■ **Subject-Verb Agreement, Commas (To Separate Nonrestrictive Clauses), Using the Right Word**

The green parts of plants has chlorophyll which traps energy from the son.

■ **Singular Possessive, Run-On Sentence, Double Negative**

A plants roots take in water from the soil a plant cannot live without no water.

Proofreading Sentences: Art and Music

■ **Subject-Verb Agreement, Using the Right Word**

Art and music allows people to express there feelings.

■ **Comma Splice, Verb Tense, Using the Right Word**

Some people create art or music for fun, other people did it as an career.

■ **Plurals (Noncount Nouns), Commas (In a Series), End Punctuation**

Musicians write musics sing songs or play instruments, don't they

■ **Subject-Verb Agreement, Capitalization**

Do you know anyone who play the french horn or the english horn?

■ **Double Subject, Using the Right Word, Colon (Introducing a List)**

Some artists they create they're pieces in the following ways painting, drawing, sculpting, and pottery making.

Proofreading Sentences: Geography

■ **Plurals, Capitalization, Commas (In Compound Sentences)**

The citys of San Francisco and Los Angeles are on the Pacific ocean and the citys of Boston and Miami are on the Atlantic ocean.

■ **Using the Right Word, Subject-Verb Agreement, Capitalization**

Their are a lot of snow in the Austrian alps.

■ **Using the Right Word, Capitalization**

The Sahara Dessert is located in the Continent of Africa.

■ **Subject-Verb Agreement, Sentence Fragment, Using the Right Word**

Natives from the Pacific Islands travels in canoes. From island too island.

■ **Capitalization, Commas (To Separate Introductory Clauses), Irregular Verb (Past Tense)**

So his family could live on the Yangtze river in China the man builded a houseboat.

Proofreading Sentences: U.S. Geography

■ **Numbers, Run-On Sentence**

There are fifty states in the United States however, Alaska

and Hawaii are not connected to the other forty-eight states.

■ **Adjectives (Superlative), Commas (In Compound Sentences), Capitalization**

Alaska is the most biggest state in size and Rhode island is

the most smallest state in size.

■ **Using the Right Word, Capitalization, End Punctuation**

Is you're favorite state East or West of the Mississippi River

■ **Commas (To Separate Introductory Phrases), Irregular Verb (Past Tense), Commas (In Addresses)**

Because of the harsh winter in New York my family taked a

winter vacation to Orlando Florida.

■ **Commas (In a Series), Numbers, Capitalization**

Lake Superior Lake Michigan and Lake Huron are 3 of the

Great lakes.

Proofreading Sentences: Earth Search

■ **Capitalization, Subject-Verb Agreement, Using the Right Word**

Some parts of planet earth has not been explored because they are quiet remote. (Remote means "hard to get to.")

■ **Adjectives (Superlative), Colon (Introducing a List), Commas (Items in a Series)**

Here are some of the world's most remotest areas parts of the Amazon jungles the Greenland ice cap and northwest Siberia.

■ **Quotation Marks, Using the Right Word, Punctuation (Period)**

Explorers usually go too remote areas for scientific study, said Ms Gordon.

■ **Plural Possessive, Commas (To Separate Introductory Phrases)**

By studying the oceans floors scientists will decide if people can live underwater.

■ **Plurals, Verb Tense, End Punctuation**

Would you like to travel to underwater citys and ate seaweed sandwiches

Proofreading Sentences: Earth Facts

■ **Singular Possessive, Using the Right Word, Capitalization**

Did you no that the glaciers of antarctica and greenland contain most of the worlds fresh water?

■ **Commas (To Set Off Appositives), Singular Possessive, Numbers**

Mount Everest earths highest peak has winds that reach two hundred miles per hour.

■ **Commas (In a Series), Subject-Verb Agreement**

Italy Japan and Chile has earthquakes and volcanic eruptions.

■ **Sentence Combining, Capitalization**

Earthquakes occur in this country. They occur on the west coast.

■ **Using the Right Word, Sentence Fragment**

Sum experts say the earth is like an top. Because it spins.

Proofreading Sentences: Greece

■ **Commas (To Set Off Appositives), Capitalization, Comma Splice**

Greece a European country juts into the Mediterranean sea, it is a peninsula country.

■ **Subject-Verb Agreement, Commas (In Compound Sentences), Capitalization**

Greece also include many little islands and two of those islands are rhodes and kos.

■ **Commas (In Numbers), Run-On Sentence, Using the Right Word**

Greece originated about 2500 years ago this small country was once an center of culture.

■ **Capitalization, Using the Right Word, Parallelism**

Many greeks earn there living by farming or to fish.

■ **Numbers, Sentence Fragment**

Greece is fifty thousand one hundred square miles in area. Just a little larger than the state of New York.

Proofreading Sentences: Ghana

■ **Commas (To Set Off Appositives), Capitalization**

Ghana a small country in western africa is a tropical country.

■ **Contractions, Subject-Verb Agreement, Commas (In a Series)**

Doesnt Ghana contains deposits of gold diamonds and bauxite?

■ **Using the Right Word, Capitalization, Comma Splice**

It's official name is the republic of Ghana, Accra is the capital city.

■ **Capitalization, Subject-Verb Agreement, Numbers**

The africans in Ghana belongs to about one hundred different ethnic groups.

■ **Sentence Fragment, Irregular Verb (Past Tense), Using the Right Word**

Ghana was known as the Gold Coast. Until it taked it's current name.

Proofreading Sentences: Great Britain

■ **Commas (To Set Off Appositives), Using the Right Word, Capitalization**

Great Britain an small island country is located off the coast of Northwestern Europe.

■ **Commas (To Separate Introductory Phrases), Capitalization, Singular Possessive**

Throughout modern history Great Britain has been one of the Worlds most powerful countries.

■ **Numbers, Colon (Introducing a List), Capitalization**

Great Britain is really the combination of 4 countries England, northern Ireland, Scotland, and Wales.

■ **Singular Possessive, Sentence Fragment, Capitalization**

One of Great Britains closest neighbors is France. Separated only by the English channel.

■ **Commas (In Compound Sentences), Contractions, Using the Right Word**

Queen Elizabeth II fulfills the roll of head of state but she doesnt really run the government.

Proofreading Sentences: Thailand

■ **Commas (To Set Off Appositives), Subject-Verb Agreement**

Thailand a country in Southeast Asia have many rivers, forests, and mountains.

■ **Capitalization, Sentence Fragment, Irregular Verb (Past Tense)**

The Country was called Siam until 1939. When it become Thailand.

■ **Plurals, Comma Splice, Adjectives (Superlative)**

More and more Thai people are moving to the citys, Bangkok is the most large city.

■ **Using the Right Word, Commas (In a Series), Parallelism**

Many Thai people make there incomes by fishing lumbering and to work in the mines.

■ **Using the Right Word, Commas (To Set Off Appositives)**

Rural Thais where the *panung* a colorful cotton or silk garment.

Proofreading Sentences: Television

■ **Commas (To Set Off Interruptions), Numbers**

Not surprisingly about ninety-nine percent of the homes in the United States have a television.

■ **Using the Right Word, Run-On Sentence, Contractions**

On the average, TV's are used four more than seven hours a day thats a lot of television viewing!

■ **Using the Right Word, Sentence Fragment, Plurals**

Commercial television stationes cell advertising time. To help pay for their costs.

■ **Commas (To Separate Introductory Phrases), Subject-Verb Agreement, Capitalization**

In addition to commercial stations there is also Public, Cable, and satellite stations.

■ **Plurals, Comma Splice, Commas (In a Series)**

Commercial television station's broadcast entertaining shows, comedies soap operas and action dramas are popular commercial shows.

Proofreading Sentences: First Aid

■ **Commas (To Separate Introductory Clauses), Sentence Fragment**

When people apply first aid they give care to someone who

is ill. Or to someone who is involved in an accident.

■ **Singular Possessive, Commas (In a Series)**

Effective first aid can save someones life, especially   the

person is bleeding poisoned or unable to breathe.

■ **Using the Right Word, Comma Splice, Capitalization**

Its important to have training before trying first aid, the

american red cross gives training.

■ **Commas (To Separate Introductory Clauses), Contractions,
Using the Right Word**

If someone is seriously hurt dont allow the person too move

around.

■ **Double Negative, Using the Right Word**

Don't give no food or water to someone which may need

surgery.

Proofreading Sentences: Fish

■ **Punctuation (Period), Quotation Marks, Using the Right Word, Capitalization**

Ms Jones said, your going to learn about fish, the most common type of animal with a backbone.

■ **Adjectives (Superlative), Capitalization, Sentence Fragment**

The most small fish is the pygmy goby of the philippines. Which grows to about one-half inch in length.

■ **Irregular Verb (Past Tense), Contractions, Comma Splice**

Fish are finded almost anywhere theres water, fish survive in either hot or cold water.

■ **Plurals, Commas (In Compound Sentences), Using the Right Word**

Most fishs never leave the water yet one species can survive for sum time in dry riverbeds.

■ **Subject-Verb Agreement, Using the Right Word, Colons**

All fish has too features in common They have a backbone and breathe through their gills.

Proofreading Sentences: School Life

■ **Contractions, Comma Splice, Plurals (Noncount Nouns)**

Im really mad, I have a lot of homeworks to do tonight.

■ **Irregular Verb (Past Tense), Plurals, Commas (In Compound Sentences), Pronoun-Antecedent Agreement**

I eated two hot dog for lunch but it did not fill me up.

■ **Numbers, Commas (To Separate Introductory Clauses), Double Negative**

Because I felt ill during my first 2 classes I didn't get no

work done on my assignments.

■ **Irregular Verb (Past Tense), Commas (In Compound Sentences), Pronoun-Antecedent Agreement**

We singed one new ballad in chorus but we didn't like them

as much as the old ballads.

■ **Plurals (Noncount Nouns), Run-On Sentence, Numbers**

The furnitures in my homeroom is too old my desk looks

one hundred years old.